21009 5635

D0120427

Funny Man

Eric Morecambe

by

Gary Morecambe

METHUEN

First published 1982 by
Methuen London Ltd
11 New Fetter Lane, London EC4P 4EE

Filmset, printed and bound in Great Britain by
Hazell Watson & Viney Ltd, Aylesbury, Bucks

ISBN 0 413 51300 9

My thanks to John Simpson
for his photographs of my father.

This book is dedicated to my wife Tracey.

Contents

Preface   9
1. Son and Father   13
2. Husband   30
3. At Home   50
4. At Work   76
5. On Holiday   92
6. Illness   107
7. Friends   118
8. Hobbies   132
9. Questions and Answers   146
Epilogue   156

Preface

My full name is Gary Trevor Bartholomew, and I am the son of a popular comedian whose real name is John Eric Bartholomew. I was born in a Middlesex hospital at 3.00 pm on Saturday, 21 April, 1956, on the same day, in fact, that my father was making the first of many appearances on the Winifred Atwell series for ATV. He says that at least something came out well that day.

Trying to picture the earlier years of our relationship is very difficult as he spent a good deal of that time touring. I have a mental picture of a man in an overcoat eating a fast meal and waving goodbye to his family, and with a smile on his face, off he would go again for another few weeks. I have always thought that it must have been of some concern to him to have missed so much of my growing up, but he insists that I never did grow up, and that he is quite willing to sit back and watch it happen now.

This book is the story of the private events that have surrounded my father, Eric Morecambe, during my lifetime. Who, other than the closest family, really knows what happens after a show, when the audience have drifted back to their homes? And who is the man behind those spectacles, whose hobby is hobbies, and who enjoys his days of leisure fishing and playing with a video recorder? In my twenty-six years, I have been witness to many of the struggles, failures and successes of his career. I have experienced, often at first hand, the emotional, temperamental and happy and sad moods and moments. As a family unit, something that we have been fortunate enough to maintain, we are left basically unscathed by the passing triumphs and tribulations. Through these pages I have attempted to unveil many of the circumstances that I have observed in my lifetime, as a member of the Morecambe family.

G.M.

HORSESHOES COTTAGE.   - - -   JANUARY I6th, I98I.

Dear Dad,

How are things witn you?

Tracey and I have decided that we must make a point to come down and visit you both soon. It's been ages since we've been able to get together! Tracey has the wedding photos in album form now, so is quite excited about showing them to mum. They have come out really well so we're both extremely pleased. The album must have cost Sheila a fortune, let alone the wedding itself!

How'xs my'horrible'brother? I really miss him since I left home. In fact, I miss him as much as possible. Gail and Paul plus family are keeping in good health, and business is picking up after a rather drab and boring start to the year.

Other than wishing to write to you for contact sake, I do have an ulterior motive. I have an idea for a book which I'd appreciate your opinion on. The book will be entitled, ERIC THROUGH THE LOOKING GLASS, and will be basically your biograpxhy but as seen through my eyes over my lifetime to date. Enclosed is the preface. could you have a read and then return it with your opinions (if printable). Thanx.

By the way, congratulations on the completion of your novel, Mr. LOnely. When is it going to be published? We can't wait for a free copy. (I can't wait for a free anything).

Hope to hear from you shortly dad,

love as always,

P.S. Excuse the typing, but it's one hell of a lot better than my writing!

S.S. HEADQUARTERS.

BERLIN.

1941.

DEAR GARY,

IT MAY BE A MISTAKE ON THE POSTMANS PART, BUT I HAVE JUST RECIEVED A LETTER FROM YOU, ALBEIT A BEGGING LETTER, NEVER THE LESS A LETTER. DO YOU REALIZE ITS THE FIRST ONE YOU'VE EVER WRITTEN TO ME AND YOU ARE NOW OVER SEVENTY THREE?.

IT'S BEEN SUCH A SHOCK TO YOUR MOTHER, SHE'S THINKING OF JOINING ME IN THIS INTENSIVE CARE UNIT! BEING A PROUD DAD, I LIKE THE IDEA OF YOUR BOOK, " ERIC THROUGH THE LOOKING GLASS " ITS BETTER THAT DES'O '.. I CANT REMEMBER HIS OTHER NAME,'THROUGH THE LOOKING GLASS' . I'LL HAVE A LOOK AT YOUR PREFACE AND LET YOU KNOW WHAT I THINK OF IT SO FAR... RUBBISH!

REGARDS MY BOOK MR. LONELY, NO YOU CANT HAVE A FREE COPY. BUT I'LL TREAT YOU LIKE I DID YOUR MUM, I'LL LET YOU HAVE ONE FOR HALF PRICE.

GIVE TRACEY MY LOVE, TELLHER I'M LOOKING FORWARD TO SEEING HER SOON.

LOVE.

P.S. YOU SIGN OFF YOUR LETTER SAYING I'LL SEE YOU SHORTLY DAD, I'LL HAVE YOU KNOW I'M NOT YOUR SHORTLY DAD, I'M YOUR TALLY DAD.

P.P.S. FOR TALLY READ TALLIE.

I I

1

Son and Father

In the autumn of 1958 my parents, along with Ernie Wise and his wife Doreen, headed down under for a tour of Australia. My sister Gail – then five years old and looking and acting more like her father each day – and I, aged two-and-a-half, were passed into the kind hands of my grandparents on my father's side, Sadie and George. We saw them quite regularly, but this was to be a stay of nearly six months. In their lifetimes they rarely left the borders of Lancashire, and since the birth of my father had only moved home once, and this was a mere four miles down the road.

Like all true Lancastrians, they were characters in the extreme. My Dad has a great deal of Sadie in him. She was sharp, aggressive and possessed a strong sense of humour. Her delight in her son's success was total. She always referred to him as 'our Eric', and many were the times she would sit Gail and me down and tell us story after story about his mischievous childhood. There was a time when he was no more than four or five years old, when he wandered from home to a building site and tap-danced for the brickies while they threw coins into his cap. And once when he was playing cowboys and indians with his cousin, 'our Sonny', Sadie had found him hanging from a rope dangling from a tree in the garden. Sonny had tried to hang him, but a bit too realistically, and left him there slowly turning purple with

Eric Bartholomew, aged eleven months.

his tongue hanging out. Sonny and Dad were inseparable friends, Sonny robust and rosy-cheeked, while Dad was pale and angelic-looking. Sonny, inevitably, was the one who got the blame for any mischief and the one who took the punishment, although they were both banned from the local cinema after being caught, while watching a film in the circle, using a pea-shooter on any bald head they could spot in the stalls.

George was a quiet and easily-contented man who was happy with the simple things life had given him, such as my Dad. Tall and handsome in his youth, he had a smile and a wit that would blossom in the company of his grandchildren. Most of his life had been spent working on a permanent market site in Morecambe. He did not have the quick brain of Sadie, but possessed a similar sense of humour. In his later life cataracts of the eyes caused him much anguish and eventually complete loss of vision after an operation proved unsuccessful. One Christmas, about the time when his eyesight was reaching its lowest level, I sent him a present. He rang to thank me for it on Boxing Day. He complained however that the liquid contents tasted like 'bloody poison'. So it should have done; it was aftershave he had been drinking.

Dad remembers making close observations on them as my grandparents. 'They thought Gary had a very big appetite. "You can't want 'seconds' after all you've just eaten?" my mother would say. But amongst all their crockery they didn't possess any full-size main-course dishes. Therefore all meals were served on smaller breakfast plates. We did explain to them that at home Gary ate off bigger plates, but I don't think they ever appreciated it.'

Both Sadie and George had contributed much behind the scenes to make Eric Bartholomew a success. Just listening to Sadie's proud memories, I cannot imagine that they ever doubted that one day he would be a star. During and after my Dad's brief schooling, which mainly derived from his lack of academic interest, Sadie worked extremely hard to find enough money to pay for his dancing, singing and piano lessons. As a pupil, Sadie had said he was a dreamboat, who would merrily while away the hours twiddling his thumbs and making ink pellets. But the music and dancing lessons gave him new interest. I asked him recently if all her efforts had been worthwhile. He replied, 'I can't play a note, can just about dance and can't sing in tune.' He scratched the back of his head and laughed. 'Yes, I suppose it was all worthwhile.'

Young Eric Bartholomew's musical failures were not the only cause of disappointment. Even his grandmother remarked, on seeing him after his birth, 'He's so small and quiet, you won't be hearing much out of this one.' How wrong they all were. He was boisterous and mischievous as a child, and not just in the early days with his cousin Sonny. He told me of his old school mates, Stanhope Milligan, Billy Lee and Eric Burton. The four of them had a secret hut where they would meet for smoking sessions. Dad would pinch his father's Woodbine dog-ends out of the ashtray and take them to the hut where they would distribute the small amount of tobacco and wrap paper around each portion, so producing a makeshift cigarette. After smoking themselves sick, they would then melt down a candle and break it up into little wads, and chew on it for hours on end as if it were a piece of chewing gum!

He was no better in the early days with Ernie. This was when they were youngsters working on one of the Bryan Michie Discovery Shows, which was where their professional career started. Dad told me, 'Ernie was very angelic and would never consider smoking. He was so good that if he earned five shillings, it would have been five-and-six by the end of the week, with the interest he would have made on it.' When they had finished their spot on stage, Dad would tell Sadie and Ernie that he was just nipping downstairs to the toilet. He would lock himself in there and puff away on some cigars called King Six, sending clouds of dark and strong-smelling smoke up the corridor. When he ran out of cigars he would settle for smoking cinnamon sticks – a little different from the expensive cigars he is seen with today.

To return to my story: on my parents' return from Australia we moved to a rented house in Blackpool, where Dad and Ernie were appearing at the central pier. Later we moved back to our flat in North Finchley. We continued visiting Morecambe regularly, often combining the trip with

16

theatre appearances. Dad would usually squeeze some fishing in with his father, a pastime they shared for many years.

George died at home in 1976. Although not unexpected, it was still a great shock for Dad, who was immensely upset. George had been eating his supper in front of the television, stood up to go into the kitchen, and collapsed and died before he touched the floor. Sadie came to live with us for a time but eventually returned home to face living alone. She moved to a small bungalow, but by this time was in poor health and spent two periods of several weeks in hospital. It was while convalescing with us at our home that Sadie took a turn for the worse and, with Mum and Dad at her bedside, she died.

I came back from work that night, having heard that she had died in the morning, to find Dad sitting in front of the television, seemingly resilient to change. It could have been

Mum, Gail, George, Sadie and me (aged nine) — one of Dad's early photo essays.

any day in any week. 'I am sorry about Sadie, Dad,' I said as I bent forward to kiss him unashamedly on the cheek, probably for the first time in many years. Later that night he cried like a lost child, and for nearly a year afterwards he would often have dreams about his parents or talk about memories concerning them. He often told me how much he missed them and how, by imitating his father's voice shouting 'Sadie', he could almost picture George standing beside him.

He recalls: 'The day after Sadie's death we had to make arrangements to have her body transported to Morecambe, where she wished to be buried, with George. It was finally decided that Mike (my driver) and myself should put the coffin in the back of the Volvo estate car, and take her up the motorway ourselves. I must confess that I fall about laughing when I think about this now, purely and simply because I know she would have fallen about laughing if she could have seen us. If I believed that she was sitting on a cloud holding hands with my Dad, looking down on us, at that time she would have been saying, "Look at that silly bugger down there." '

I asked him what he could remember of the last years of being with them. 'I think it was after George's death that I became more aware about them. When he died my mother wanted to die. She wished to be with my father. She believed that he was up in heaven awaiting her arrival. I knew that all she had and all that meant so much to her was now gone. She had never been a church-goer as such, but she was a strong believer in the Christian faith, and I think that having that belief helped her through the last eighteen months after George's death.'

Obviously my Dad's feelings for and memories of his parents are as vivid, as wonderful and as enduring as are mine for him. But he is also a pretty unusual father! As a child, I saw him as an affectionate stranger whom I often

Youca...

My Dear Evie.

Many Thanks for reg. Letter + also Letter This morning. Well Love you will soon be 21 + enclosed is £10·0·0 + Pop + I wish you a very happy Birthday + we will be thinking of you on the 14th. I am sending you a Birthday Cake to This address + Mary from Kilburn's is sending you 21 bars of rock which she promised you. Before I write any more in This Letter I want to Thank you for being a good boy to us + not bringing us any trouble. I know at times you have thought me hard but I have had to do it for your own benefit. Now you are your own boss + I sincerely hope you have learned a little from my nagging. I don't want to be sentimental but I just want you to know how we both have loved you + tried to do our best for you as you know we always wanted you to have only the best, + though now to the world you are a man, to us you will always be our baby (so don't get any big ideas). From now on I do not interfere with whatever you do, but if you want advice well of course we will be there. We wish you Good Luck, Good Health + Prosperity + remember the world is yours for a football + may you score many goals. So I close now + once again saying "Thank you Evie" for giving us so many happy memories + causing us no worries — may the Sun always shine for you. love. God Bless You. From Your Loving Mam + Pop
xxxx x xx xx x x xxxx xx xxx

Sadie's letter to Dad on his twenty-first birthday.

loved and feared. Now I know him better, love him just as much, but see the other, more temperamental side of him that his audience is never shown. After all, the warm, gentle comedian that the public loves must have other sides of his character too, and in extracting the appealing aspects of the public person, sometimes the family man was left a bit short of patience and even time. My father is no doubt an artiste of the highest order, maybe a comic genius. The constant demands upon him, however, can make him lacking in tolerance and sometimes irrational. At these times something of minor importance can take on exaggerated proportions and worry him enormously. But my mother usually puts things into their proper perspective, setting his mind at ease. An admirable quality with my father is that he sees his own faults so clearly and appreciates my mother's help.

I will always remember the first serious encounter I had with the less tolerant side of his nature: I was only nine at the time, and it was during the period, in the sixties, when he had begun to develop a fondness for gadgetry and gimmicky things. At this time a reel-to-reel tape machine, a battery-operated portable cassette machine and an early form of stereo record-player sufficed his needs. These items, amongst the jungle of books, files and pencils, he kept in his study. Although not forbidden, Gail and I were discouraged from entering this shrine. One day my mother was visiting relations and Dad had taken himself off on a long walk. Gail was contenting herself playing upstairs in her bedroom, and partly out of boredom and curiosity, it seemed an appropriate moment to explore the forbidden study. Only a few minutes were required to unwind some of the tape from one of his many cassettes. The damage was minimal so I was not exactly overconcerned. Not realizing how important that particular tape was, I shoved the damaged reel deep into the nearest open drawer and fled.

At about midday he returned. It is strange how things

work out, for as if he had been alerted in some strange way that I had been rummaging in his study, the first thing he did was to go in there to listen to that particular tape. His chin must have struck the ground firmly when he slid open the oak drawer. Gail was in her bedroom still and I was now in my own room too, further down the corridor. A feeling of 'living is so easy' and 'with us so secure' was soon shattered by the slamming door and resounding echoes that flowed throughout the house, followed by fast-approaching heavy thuds as Dad bounded up the staircase. I felt a nervous sickness in my stomach as it occurred to me that I might have to shoulder some of the responsibility for what had happened. This attitude seemed very generous to me at the age of nine. Normally somebody else shouldered responsibility, but with no mother about, there was no one to bail me out and it looked as if I would have to face the music. Firstly he entered Gail's room and I could pick up muffled shouting followed by crying. He strongly resembled John Cleese's portrayal of Basil Fawlty as he subsequently burst in upon my room. I felt a little giddy as he started to shake me, and it was not too long before I was also crying. The situation ended relatively peacefully, with him fetching Gail and hugging us both, laughing and crying at the same time. I never did confess to damaging his tape, but instead unsuccessfully tried to shift the blame to a neighbourhood friend!

Our relationship is a paradoxical one – Dad and I are extremely close and yet I can never quite relax with him. We do not have a straightforward father-and-son relationship – he is too unpredictable for that. Sometimes I think of him more as a favourite uncle, slightly disconnected from the family but thought a lot of. Of course, much of that feeling probably relates to my having had to share him with the public all my life.

One thing I have learnt with my father over the years –

Dad with Gail; success just around the corner.

as have my mother and sister, and as eventually will my younger brother, Stevie — is never to try and compete with him, especially when in company. And, by the same token, always to let him have the last word. These aspects of his character stem directly from his work, which demands so much from him that he needs a degree of tolerance in his domestic life. It was not until I became older that I realized he has a deep sense of insecurity. It was this, more than ego, which made him discourage family competition.

When in company, we (one of the family) become the straight man, temporarily taking over Ernie's role. A good example is a cocktail party we held a few years ago, to celebrate my parents' silver wedding anniversary. As I mingled and filled up the semi-drained champagne glasses, it occurred to me that someone should say a few words of congratulations and toast their health. As my eyes travelled the room in search of a person to carry out this informal act, it dawned on me that I was the one to do it. Although my Dad and I have a number of things in common, one thing I do not share with him is a love of talking in public. Nevertheless I nervously cleared my throat and said loudly, 'Can I have your attention, everybody.' I hoped that the acidic bubbly inside me would take over.

'Quiet . . . Shush . . . Gary's going to speak,' came echoing voices. Silence fell.

'I would just like to say . . . propose a toast, to my mother and father (pause) whom I have known all my life.'

That brought an appreciative burst of laughter. Then in stepped Dad. 'That's the first time I've heard him speak since I've known him – and he almost made a joke.'

That brought a big laugh and I felt myself burn just a touch. 'Thank you, Dad,' I continued.

'Did you speak again?' he shouted in mock seriousness.

'Anyway,' I persevered, 'I'd just like to congratulate them on their twenty-fifth wedding anniversary.'

Everyone raised their glasses and a nonsensical gathering of voices returned in a powerful wave. Still blushing, I thankfully lost myself in the crowd, prickling still at Dad's interruption but admiring his gift for ad-libbing.

Two further episodes emphasize his use of this gift.

When I was at Aldenham School, Dad would often make guest appearances. He did this solely for my popularity and happiness and for that effort I am eternally grateful. I was a touch apprehensive, though, when he accepted an invitation to give some of the prizes away on the parents' visitation-day ceremony. This required more of him than just being there. I need not have concerned myself, however. He was brilliant. Having given all the cups out and slapped a few of the faces, as he would Ernie's, he walked up to the wooden table which had supported those cups and casually handed it out to one of the masters, as though it were one of the awards. He had a marvellous time and everyone was highly appreciative of his efforts.

The other ad-libbing story occurred shortly after he had guested in a question and answer session, at Haberdasher's School, two miles from Aldenham. He recalled: 'One of the boys sitting in the front row was a typical "brainbox" type. You always find one in every school. He obviously wasn't impressed that I made a living out of being a comedian, because after about half an hour he raised his arm to pose a question. "Tell me, Mr Morecambe, do you ever look at yourself seriously at times and feel that perhaps you are a bit of a fool?" Those were almost his exact words. You rotten little devil, I thought, and then replied, "Yes, I suppose I sometimes do. As I sit in the garden at my luxury home, sipping long drinks by the swimming pool or driving around in my Rolls Royce, yes, I suppose I do feel a bit of a fool." That was marvellous. Everyone began laughing and the "brainbox" didn't ask another question throughout the sitting.'

When I left school I persevered with a two-year business studies course in St Albans. At the college's request, Dad came over one evening to do another one of those question and answer sessions, in a similar vein to the one at Haberdasher's. This one was not for students, however, but for the lecturers, their wives and relatives. The escaping laughter and chatter my parents heard as they made their way across to the college hall came to an abrupt halt as they made their entrance. Ironically, and due probably to the fact that they doubted Dad would accept their invitation, the audience now found itself far more nervous and apprehensive than *he* was. Before Dad was to face the questions, a dinner had been arranged. A long table, surrounded by the silent, nervous people, awaited my mother and him. 'For one awful moment we were slightly unnerved by what appeared to be an evening spent with an audience gripped by rigor mortis,' recalls Dad. The officiator led them to their places of honour at the table and they silently seated themselves. Then nothing much happened for the next few seconds as they were probably waiting for my parents to commence eating. Dad decided he had had enough of this, and so, with hands hidden beneath the table, began loudly to applaud himself and then smiled to acknowledge the applause, as though he had nothing to do with it. This started a small avalanche of applause which led him to stand up and take a bow. The ice had been broken and the evening went on to be a big success.

I quite often have the desire to ask Mum how Dad feels about me as a son. Have I been a good son? Was I any trouble to him at any period in his life? I can only presume (accepting that I have no more peculiarities than most, have never been a drug addict and have not got a criminal record) that the only stage of my life when perhaps I was a burden to my parents was during my late teens. As with most teenagers, everything I warmed to and identified with was of necessity anti-social. Clothes in particular had to be scruffy and my hair was long enough to keep my shoulders warm. I even had one of my ears pierced and a gold sleeper ear-ring inserted. I walked into the house on the evening I had had it pierced; Dad was standing by the kitchen sink, talking to my mother. I slowly turned my head and pulled back the curtain of hair.

'Look, I've had my ear pierced,' I said proudly, thinking it would upset them.

My mother expressed a little concern, which pleased me. Dad took one look and burst into mock-hysterical laughter. 'No, no, I think it's really good,' he said, still deliberately sniggering from behind his hand. 'Tell me, did they put the ring in so that you can hang yourself up at night in the cupboard?' He fell about laughing at his own joke, taking some of the edge off my achievement.

My teenage rebellion passed as predictably as most, but with my mother having to bear the brunt of my tiresomeness as Dad was often away doing shows. The night I returned home late after a visit to the pub, ignoring my mother's waving figure in the garden, to tumble into bed, was one such occasion. She informed me in the morning that there had been a fire in the paddock which she had been forced, clad in nightie and slippers, to put out single-handedly.

Another time, returning from a party in my ageing Morris 1300, I managed to drive it off the road, turn it over and nearly write both it and myself off in one fell swoop. A friend helped me and my battered vehicle home and this time I was glad of Dad's absence to mutter soothing words to Mum, who was waiting up in bed, before I retired. Unfortunately Dad returned the following morning and so I decided to slip out of the house early to allow him a cooling-off period. He needed it. When I came back he aired his feelings pretty openly. As I understood it, he was not going to communicate with me for the next week. And he kept his word. But after that he did help me to get the car repaired and back on the road within a month.

The adoption of my brother Stevie has been particularly interesting in the light of my Dad's temperament. As a child – and also as a man – I have always stood down to my Dad's sudden outbursts. I would do anything to calm him down and not upset him, whether it meant apologizing or shutting up. Stevie officially joined the family at the age of four, introduced to us by Gail who was working as a nursery nurse at the time. He had very little vocabulary – although he knew all the swearwords – and was frustrated at not being able to express himself. As soon as he could string a few sentences together we realized there would be confrontation problems between him and Dad. Neither of them would stand down to one another. Stevie had a temper and would shout back at Dad as loudly and as violently as the mood took him – quite the opposite to myself as a child in every way. Fortunately Stevie's temper has lessened as he has grown older and become secure. He no longer aggravates Dad unnecessarily, and has become more reserved and respectful in his attitude. In all fairness to Stevie, Dad is slightly misplaced in the role of the man willing to take on an adopted son and go to lengths to help him settle in. He loves Stevie just as he loves Gail and me, but his attitude is more of acceptance than perseverance. He was delighted to have Stevie brought up as a Bartholomew, on equal terms with Gail and me, and he begrudges him nothing, but always saw the upbringing and sorting out of problems as my mother's responsibility.

The best part is that we really are a close family, and our relationship has developed in recent years. Stevie in many ways has established himself as the biggest character of us all.

<u>HORSESHOES</u>.

Dera (that was a gᵒod start), Tallie Dad,

Thankyou for your swift reply to my letter! I'm so pleased to hear (or read),
that you find the idea appealing.

The postman tells me he had to go through murder to climb over the'wall' to deliver
the letter to you. He agrees that it was all worthwhile, however, ᴀɴᴅxᴀᴀ but
demands a free copy when released.

Well now you can cast your eyes over the first chapter which I have just completed.
I hope you like it. It seems so boring covering the early years as I remember
so little ᴀf about them. You were never at home until ᴀ I was fifty one!

ᴀ Write back soon, as I'd love to know how you think it's going.

See you when I can next escape from Cambridge,

                              Love *Garyll*

DEAR SON,

HAVING READ YOUR FIRST CHAPTER, I CAN SEE THAT THE MILLION AND A HALF POUNDS I
SPENT ON YOUR EDUCATION WAS'NT ENTIRELY MISPLACED. I WAS THRILLED TO SEE THAT YOU
COULD SPELL ' MORECAMBE ' TH E PAPER RIGHT WAY. MOST PEOPLE SPELL IT WRONG, THESE ARE
JUST A FEW WAYS..... ' MORECOMBE '.... ' MORCOM '..... MORECOMB...... MORKUM... AS
A MATTER OF FACT IN AMERICA THEY PRONOUNCE IT ' MORYCAMBY AND WISE. ' AND IN AN
AFRICAN PAPER TH M CALLED US ' ERIC MORE — CAMBY AND ERINE WISE ' ANOTHER PAPER CALL-
ED US , ERIC MORCOM AND RENE RICE . BUT WE'VE LEARNED TO LIVE WITH IT. THE LATE
ED. SULLIVAN ONCE ANNOUNCED JEWEL AND WARRISS AS JEWELS AND HIS WALRUSS, HONESTLY....
HOWEVER!

I LIKED MOST OF WHAT I READ, ALREADY I'VE BECOME VERY FOND OF THE HERO.
BUT YOU MUST BE CAREFUL WHAT YOU SAY ABOUT OTHER PEOPLE, YOU MUST'NT HURT ANYONES
FEELINGS, AFTER ALL ITS SOPPOSED TO BE A HAPPY BOOK, NOT A TRUE BRITT. SOME OF THE
PEOPLE YOU MENTION ARE MAY FRIENDS AND I WOULD LIKE THEM TO STAY THAT WAY.

KEEP IT UP,

ITS NEVER EASY. I'LL SHOW IT TO YOUR MOTHER WHEN I THINK SHE'S FIT ENOUGH. SHE SENDS
HER LOVE. GIVE OUR LOVE TO ALL MY FAMILY AROUND CAMBRIDGE.

) RD X

PS. LAST NIGHT YOUR MOTHER SAW A VISION.... ME.

2

Husband

Being the one privileged to voice his feelings throughout the pages of this book does not mean that I am the one closest to or the most knowledgeable on my subject. That honour must obviously go to my mother, Joan, who has protected, aided, controlled and generally taken care of Dad through the years they have been together. And as Dad would say, not necessarily in that order. She really does understand what makes him tick, and how to assist him in the daily problems without mothering or suffocating him, which he would find intolerable. As she says, he needs protecting from himself.

Their relationship is a strong, practical and secure one, but, as with all my father's relationships, it has been influenced by his work and his touch of eccentricity and genius. His job and his public manner have, I think, inhibited the open expression of their commitment to each other. Dad demands a lot of love and attention, but is not always willing to express his fondness for his wife. Also my mother hides her response by not allowing her feelings to be shown. In many ways she has to act as much as he does in keeping up the public image as his wife. But I know they are very happy together and have grown happier as the pressures of life seem to be easing up a little.

My mother first met Dad in Edinburgh in the very early

fifties. In those days he was touring successfully with Ernie, as a variety double act, working every day of the week and travelling by train on Sundays to a new destination. Mum was dabbling in showbusiness herself as a soubrette, the name given to one of the general dog's bodies in showbiz. They sang a little, danced a little and worked in sketches with the comics. She went to Edinburgh to replace a showgirl who had gone down with appendicitis. Arriving at the theatre for band call, practically the first person she met was my father. As she recalls it, 'An American girl introduced us. She too was appearing in the show and had met Eric several times previously through working on the same bill as he and Ernie. I later discovered that within minutes of meeting me, Eric told her I was the girl whom he was going to marry! The next few days I couldn't escape from him, though he didn't interest me in the least except as a talented artiste. He was the last person in the world I had any intention of going steady with.'

The routine of these shows was to rise late in compensation for the late nights, then to collect your mail from the theatre, where inevitably you would meet up with a few of the company and go out for coffee. Lunch was eaten back at the digs, and most afternoons spent in the cinema before work in the evening.

Dad's pursuit of my mother was persistent and eventually she agreed to have coffee with him, though his pride was hurt when she took him round the shops to look for a present for her current boyfriend! My mother loved the humour and vitality which Eric and Ernie generated. They were enormous fun to be with. She soon learned to take more than a passing interest in Dad.

The next stop after Edinburgh was Margate, where, coincidentally, her parents and family had a hotel. It was decided that Eric and Ernie would stay there – at a much reduced rate – but soon the invitation had been extended and the majority of Billy Cotton's band had moved in too. Mother was not there at the time, but the family got on well with Eric and soon the return match to Morecambe was planned for Sadie and George to meet Joan. Sadie's comment was, 'I don't know what she sees in our Eric. It certainly can't be his money!'

As youngsters my parents were fairly impulsive and became engaged shortly after meeting each other. Mum told me: 'I presumed this was how the situation would remain and that marriage would be a long time off, due to Eric always working without a break. But as luck would have it, he had a couple of days off soon after our engagement because he and Ernie were booked for a broadcast at the London Palladium, a big step forward in their career. On the spur of the moment, during a hasty phone call, Eric said, "Doing the broadcast means that I've got a bit of time

Wedding day, 1952. The photographer was a comic too.

off and we could get married on the Sunday if arrangements can be made in time." '

My grandmother laid on a reception at the Margate hotel, a special licence was obtained and all arrangements completed within a week or so, only a few short days after Sadie and George had been told of the engagement. Apparently Sadie's sole regret was that she had not been able to change the engagement notice in the local paper to a wedding one!

The honeymoon consisted of a couple of days at the Cumberland Hotel in London; not a very romantic time as Dad was obsessed with the material for the broadcast. Commenting on the matter, he recalls, 'I wouldn't say I was obsessed with the broadcast, but what honeymoon?'

Then it was off to Sheffield for a pantomime season. This was the 'old' Sheffield which in winter seemed permanently buried beneath a cloud of smog, and it was generally a very depressing time for them. The weather was among the worst they had known, with heavy snow, smog and freezing cold. Their digs were too cold and spartan to tolerate so they moved to a comfortable bed-sit. Here they bought in their own food which a pleasant landlady cooked for them, and they had a nice open coal fire always burning in the grate.

However, very soon after getting married my mother became pregnant, which came as a shock as they had not planned on having a family for quite some while. My mother recalls, 'Carrying a baby was no pleasure during that winter in Sheffield. Morning sickness was more of an all-day sickness and from time to time, to improve my health, Eric would send me off to his parents in Morecambe for a few days, where the sea air worked wonders. All those walks along the promenade taking in gallons of fresh air. The whole atmosphere was restorative. As soon as I returned to Sheffield I would start the sickness again. However, all unpleasant things come to an end.'

The following September my sister Gail was born in

Morecambe while my father was working a summer season in Blackpool. After the season ended they resumed touring, and all the trappings that accompany a baby had to be toured with them. They did not have a permanent home as a base except for my father's parents in the north and my mother's parents in the south. It was not until they decided it was time to have a second child, hence my existence two and half years after Gail's birth, that they felt it essential to have a place of their own.

My mother has always been pleased with the rather astute way she has handled her business affairs, and recalls: 'Show people are notorious for making a mess of the business side of their careers. I have always been interested in that side of things and so took to the problem of purchasing a house on a shoe-string. We bought a run down Victorian house in North Finchley, just a walk away from the Torrington Arms which my family now ran having moved from Margate. The house was almost opposite a park and it was to be our first real home.'

During the period awaiting my arrival, Mum set about having the house converted into two flats, the ground floor one to be kept as our own, while Dad continued to tour, working as hard as ever. With a wife and shortly two children to support, it was essential to keep in work. Although totally committed to the idea of him and Ernie becoming stars, Dad almost dreaded the responsibility that finally achieving stardom would bring him. The star of the show is the one who 'carries the can' — the person the whole show revolves around and is reliant on. He was happy as second top on all the bills. In this position he had both prestige and a good salary, but not the responsibility the star has.

The advent of television not only changed their working format of endless touring (although that would still continue in moderation) but also brought a change in my Dad's attitude to success and what he felt he was able to do in

34

comedy. Radio had been a continuously successful medium for them, and they would hardly miss a chance to appear on it. My mother says, 'I've known the two of them to be touring all week, and then at weekends to rush over by train to Manchester from wherever they were playing, do a radio show and then rush back. They did many a series in this manner.'

The television break came when they were offered the series 'Running Wild'. At that time, television was terribly new and comedy on television was still very much in the experimental stage. They tackled the series eagerly as a new challenge and never once thought it would arouse much attention. They were wrong. For some reason the national press focussed on Morecambe and Wise's introduction to television as if it were an event of major national importance. When the first of the series came on, the press crucified it. My mother recalled to me, 'I had watched with great interest, of course, and thought the show was entertaining. People reading those write-ups the following day will never know just how demoralizing it was for Eric and Ernie. In just one day most of their confidence seemed destroyed. What they needed, but didn't get, was constructive criticism. It took courage to face an audience shortly afterwards. As it happened, they couldn't have had a better tonic, for on that very first stage appearance after the series, they brought the house down and received a standing ovation.

'No one was offering any more series at the time, and they wouldn't have accepted even if they were, but they did spots on other people's television shows, including the Winifred Atwell show which coincided with your birth. Your father was like a cat on hot bricks, with you about to be born and a new show to appear on that evening. It was lucky you arrived several hours earlier than expected. Eric was able to visit me and get a glimpse of you just before dashing off to the studio.'

Looking back on the whole spectrum of those years, it seems the summers, although arranged primarily around work, were an enjoyable time for all the family. We could close up the house and move to the resort where my father was appearing, and remain there for the length of my school summer holidays in a rented house often near the sea. My mother would return home when it neared the time for Gail and me to go back to our schools, and leave Dad to plod on for the final fortnight or whatever was remaining, alone. Staying at Brixham in Torquay was definitely the happiest season. My parents spent much of the time taking Gail and

What does my father do for a living?

me out for long walks and picnics, and Dad was able to join in more than on most other seasons.

Mum and Dad were also travelling abroad a fair amount by this time, as Eric and Ernie were appearing on the Ed Sullivan shows. Mum recalls: 'In 1963 we took advantage of working in the States to come home via Jamaica. We spent a week there, which should have been nothing but sheer paradise. The first three days we enjoyed the good life, and then, much to your father's disappointment, and to my dismay, I went down with food poisoning. We had a chalet-type cabin affair right on the shoreline, with all the facilities of the nearby hotel. I had little chance to wade into the sea that lapped tidelessly within feet of our door. All I wanted to do was die. Eric despairs of me on these occasions as I refuse to seek medical help. Therefore I was confronted by a rather irate doctor many hours after first contracting the illness. He had to fill me with injections and tablets which, taken earlier, would have been more effective.'

Later came the trip to Australia – three months' work in Melbourne followed by a further three in Sydney – when Gail and I were left in Sadie and George's care. One of Mum's clearest memories of Australia, probably because for years afterwards nobody knew of it, not even my father, was her near fatal attempt at swimming a little way out to sea. Winifred Atwell was topping the show Eric and Ernie were on and she had a pleasant house on the beach in Bilbao. It was a beautiful spot and one Sunday she invited my father and mother and Ernie and Doreen for a barbeque lunch on the patio. My mother takes up the story: 'I loved sports, especially swimming. I still love swimming but Eric, being a non-swimmer, is all the more wary of the possible dangers, especially where we were staying that day, as the currents are particularly strong. I felt quite confident about taking myself out for a long swim and so I left the small party having drinks and slipped into the water. I swam out strongly as I am a capable swimmer, and after a while decided I should head back as lunch was most probably ready. As I swam back I found that the coast was slipping further and further away. Then I began to feel cramp in my leg which was rather a dangerous signal. Fortunately Australian beaches are patrolled by lifeguards and so, much to my humiliation but unseen by everyone on the patio, I raised an arm and out swam a handful of the super lifesavers who towed me back to shore. I sat down for a while to recover my breath and then nonchalantly resumed my place with the others on Winifred's patio. It was much later, only a couple of years ago, while in conversation with someone at a party, that I happened to say, "I remember having once been towed in by the lifeguards in Australia." I wondered if Eric had heard me, and sure enough his ears pricked up and he started questioning me all about it. I think he was more shocked that I had been able to keep a secret from him for all those years than about the actual incident.'

Mum and Dad's memories of the early days of fame seem among their happiest. Wherever they were travelling or staying, it seems they would spend the best part of the time in convulsions. Despite Dad and Mum leading totally separate private lives from Ernie and Doreen, they did have some wonderful moments together. She remembers: 'Eric and Ernie were ever so funny together, even in private when only the four of us were talking. Ernie would make a comment about someone or something, and Eric would be straight in with a funny line.'

Apparently my father was virtually a non-drinker in the early days. It was when he started to do the ATV shows that he allowed himself to drink. Says my mother: 'To keep things in proportion, he was never a heavy drinker by any standards but it only took a few to affect him dramatically, and a need for more became greater as the pressures of working life and social events mounted. It interests me to note that he lacked the discipline to be able to cut down on his drinking, yet he disciplined himself to give it up completely.'

It has now been two years or more since he has had an alcoholic drink. During their earlier years together they did not even keep a drink in the house. It simply was not considered a part of their life. But Dad started out as a social drinker and it developed from there. Having a few drinks would give him a 'lift', but the effect would wear off, leaving him jumpy and depressed.

Dad and Ernie started the Morecambe and Wise one-night concerts in the early seventies. He began insisting on having a drink in his dressing-room, something he had never had before. After the shows, and it was the same with the television shows, he would consume a couple of large drinks very quickly. The show itself would have left him charged with the adrenalin, and the combination of excitement and alcohol went straight to his head. My mother remembers what it was like being with him then: 'Having been married to a non-drinker for so many years, and one who was proud of the fact that he wasn't one of the people who needed a drink before a performance, and then to see him change in this fashion gave me a feeling of helplessness. I didn't know how to cope with the situation. But I could sympathize with him for the pressures he was under. Don't forget also that he had had a massive heart attack in 1968 and turning to drink was a way of seeking confidence.'

My parents had a phase which they call their 'caravan era'. This came about when my father passed his driving test (first time, he would no doubt add), in 1953, just after Gail had been born. With no permanent home of their own, and Dad always having to travel, a caravan seemed the solution to their problems. But there was more to caravanning than they thought. As my mother tells it, 'Our very first journey was from Morecambe to Margate, a long journey now and an extremely long one then, without the benefit of motorways. There was a lovely site near Birchington where we intended to stay. We congratulated ourselves on a trouble-free journey too soon, for in Elstree we had a spot of bother. A very steep hill confronted us and our hearts sank as we found ourselves behind a slow, heavily-laden lorry. Eric changed down to first gear so we could take the hill but unfortunately lost too much speed and finished up stalling. Then we felt ourselves slipping backwards towards the on-coming traffic. Finally we jack-knifed across the road, nearly causing a major accident. I jumped out of the car with Gail in my arms and started shouting at the cars to stop. Eric was panicking at the wheel, but succeeded in getting the damn thing started again. A few minutes later we were up the hill, but our nerves were a little the worse for wear.'

But Dad insists, 'It was a magical piece of driving in such high-pressure conditions.'

Another caravanning incident occurred while they were in Manchester and was potentially just as dangerous. Dad and Ernie were working at the Ardwick Hippodrome and it was decided to use the caravan instead of finding digs. But on arrival they found there was nowhere to park it. They eventually got permission to leave it in the parking lot next to the Hippodrome but had not bargained on the subsequent weather conditions. 'I cannot recall having seen such torrents of rain then or since,' said my mother. 'Although we had more than enough rain water, there was no actual running water near at hand. Coping with a baby and nappy changes made it one of our less pleasant experiences.'

The weather continued to make their week wet and uncomfortable and the final straw came when my mother put a stew in the oven one evening. 'Gail was in her high chair and Eric was doing the show. Having left the stew for a while to cook, I decided to check on how it was coming along. I discovered that the gas had gone out and without stopping to think, leaned forward and struck a match. There was an almighty explosion. It was strong enough to shift the high chair a few feet and of course did me no favours. My hair caught fire but I quickly put it out, and my eyebrows and eyelashes were singed to a virtual stubble. But my overriding concern was for Gail, who thankfully was not hurt. I dread to think what would have happened had I tried to relight it half an hour or so later. It was disturbing enough for Eric as it was, coming home for a hot dinner after a tiring show to find a disturbed caravan and a dishevelled wife with a rather singed appearance!' They did not stay with caravans much longer after that, as it was apparent that caravans and Morecambes were not compatible, although there was one other memorable incident involving a caravan, and also fishing, another source of colourful memories for my mother.

My parents have a saying that everything my Dad does is tinged with humour, and it is true. They were in Blackpool one summer season and living in a caravan. The weather was particularly good that year and all was going well. An opportunity to do some fishing came about because of the interest shown by some of the bandsmen in Dad's show. He was the one with the car so he arranged to meet them at the pier where he would pick them up and take them out to the stretch of water they had decided upon visiting. They had arranged to meet at six o'clock in the morning so as to make the most of their day. None of them had finished work until late and so they were not going to have much sleep. My mother relates the story: 'Eric couldn't eat his dinner fast enough so as to get to bed, and he kept saying in between mouthfuls, "I mustn't oversleep. I've arranged to meet the lads at six o'clock." He finished eating and headed straight for bed, setting the alarm as he hurriedly undressed himself. So we went to bed and fell asleep and all was very peaceful. Suddenly I felt myself being shaken and heard Eric shouting,

The first house of their own – Harpenden, 1962.

"I've overslept! The alarm didn't go off. What shall I do now? God, I'm going to be late!"

'He calmed down and ate the cereal I had left on the table for him the night before, consuming it as quickly as he had done his supper. I let him get on with it and dropped back to sleep. A few minutes later I felt a gentle prodding on my shoulder.

' "What is it now?" I said, half asleep.

' "I didn't oversleep," he said in a whisper. "It's only four o'clock and I've eaten my Puffed Wheat."

'This meant that he had returned home at midnight, had his supper, gone to bed for three hours, and then had his breakfast. I looked at him, dressed for a day on the river in his full fishing outfit. He even had his pork pie hat on and held a fishing rod in his hand. Inwardly I could not help but laugh.

' "I can't take all the gear off again," he said.

' "You'll have to sit up against the wall then and just doze for a couple of hours," I replied as I settled down again.

'He agreed, and so, sitting next to me with his fishing rod stretched across the bed, we both fell asleep. The next thing I was aware of was awakening to find that all hell had been let loose. He was going berserk as now he really had overslept and it was eight o'clock in the morning. He charged outside, slamming the door behind him, and went off to see if his companions were still awaiting his arrival. The two of them were there all right, completely unperturbed by the fact he was so late. It became the joke of the show. They wouldn't let Eric forget that he had sat up half the night in his fishing togs, eaten his cereal at four in the morning and still been late for their date.'

Mum can also recall another fishing incident that occurred many years later with a regular fishing friend of Dad's. 'I prepared a flask of hot coffee and soup and a few sandwiches before the two of them set off. They were fishing on two consecutive days, but returning home in the evenings. On arrival at the river, Eric immediately went for a mug of coffee. The flask must have suffered a shaky journey, for as he opened the lid, the coffee exploded all over him. He had hardly had time to make himself comfortable on the bank and now he was standing there with steam rising off him, saturated. Although concerned, his friend could not help but laugh, as I would have done had I been there. They went back to the car and drove to a nearby pub where the kindly landlady offered to wash out the clothes, meanwhile lending Eric a pair of old trousers and blanket to be going on with. They refused to miss their fishing, so went back to the river, blanket wrapped around Eric and all. I was quite puzzled when they came home, seeing Eric in different and ill-fitting trousers, and with a blanket draped across his shoulders. The next day they set off to fish at the same spot. Again I prepared food and drink and ushered them out. Eric decided to walk the bank on their arrival, just to see if there was possibly a better point to fish from. He turned to Morris, saying, "That's a good spot just over there, let's take a look," and as he finished speaking he leapt with all the agility of the middle-aged man he was, straight on to what he thought was a firm mud bank. Alas, it turned out to be soggy mud, and on landing in it with both feet, he stared dejectedly at Morris as he slowly sank up to his waist. Morris was curled up on the bank and would be needing oxygen if he laughed any more. Two incidents in two days was too much for the man to cope with. So they found themselves back in the pub with the friendly landlady, who again washed out his clothes, and they spread them to dry on some bushes near the river. He came home that evening shaking his head despairingly, his damp clothes in hand, saying what we have often said before: "Why is my life always tinged with comedy?" '

Dad has never had any confidence when it comes to buying my mother a present. He was working in the States many years ago and Mum had decided not to go with him on this trip. He spent much of his time in the company of Roy and Fiona Castle who were also working over there. He told Fiona that he wanted to buy my mother a nightie but was not sure of her size (after all these years) and asked if she could help him choose one. I think he has a phobia of buying her the wrong thing. After much gagging about with the girl assistant in the store, no doubt making jokes about the different garments and so on, they bought a nightie and came away well pleased with their choice. When he returned to England and produced the garment, apparently it was the smallest thing Mum had ever seen! If he had not looked so serious as he presented it to her she would have thought it was a joke. What had happened was, with all the fun and games at the store, they had picked up the wrong one. The next time they saw Fiona, Mum said jokingly to her, 'Well Fi, you helped him choose it, so you must have it.' And would you believe it, it fitted her perfectly.

Dad complains if Mum does not tell him exactly what present she wants, whether it be for a birthday or Christmas, and then when she gives him a strong-enough hint, he takes no notice. One Christmas he knew exactly what she wanted. In fact, if he did not buy it for her, she decided, she was going to buy it herself. She told me: 'It was an attractive but practical watch that I had set my heart on. I had seen it at a jeweller's in St Albans. As it neared the twenty-fifth, I took myself off to Luton to hunt around for presents for Stevie. The agreed arrangement was that Eric would await my return before going off to St Albans to do his bits of shopping alone. When I got home, he announced casually that he had been to the shops already. I was quite impressed. "Isn't that marvellous," I thought. "He's been to St Albans, rooted out the shop and found the watch I want." Come the big day I opened up my package and discovered that he hadn't bought me the watch at all, but instead had nipped down to Harpenden and settled for a silver necklace and bracelet – without doubt very pleasant, but similar to a set he had bought me two years previously and which had hardly ever been worn. It defeated me slightly that he could go out and purchase a near replica of two items that were not my cup of tea. Mind you, I wish I hadn't hurt his feelings by passing a comment that Christmas morning. It upset him a great deal, and I felt very guilty. If he had just dropped me a hint beforehand that it wasn't the watch I don't think I would have shown my disappointment.'

He also enjoys buying himself presents and keeping it a secret from my mother. His favourite saying to both Gail and me has become: 'Don't tell your mum.' He buys himself meerschaum pipes and expensive watches, and hides them away for a while, then over a period of time starts producing them, hoping she will not notice. He enjoys keeping secrets from her by kidding himself that she would disapprove. In this way he has automatically created an excuse for being

My wedding, October 1980. Only Dad and Stevie are looking at the camera.

secretive. But this, in a similar fashion to the time he was drinking, is something that developed later in life. He was never a secretive man in their earlier years. 'What I don't like about it all,' says my mother, 'is that he makes me look the sort of woman who wants to keep her husband under her thumb. Really it doesn't matter to me what he wants to buy for himself. I just don't see the enjoyment in being secretive and telling white lies. Maybe I am a lot firmer than I used to be. With the pressures of work in the fifties, sixties and seventies, we would all try to pamper him and make sure that he was happy, often agreeing with what he said even if we knew he was in the wrong. Basically it was a desire to make life as easy as possible, so he could relax and concentrate on his profession. He deserved all the help we could give him. But now, I don't always give in to him, and I stand up for my convictions more. He is far better since I *have* begun to dig my heels in. He is a person who needs a good deal of attention and cossetting, and he will always get it. That is the psychology of the man. But he is definitely easier to live with and seems to have mellowed now that he is in his fifties. Eric was brought up in a generation during which the woman was the hub of the household. "Women's lib" was not recognized. The woman is there to be leant on at all times, and, to be honest, he hasn't done too badly having this requirement filled. But then I haven't done too badly having him for a husband, either.'

Dear dad,

The typewriter has seemingly ceased to function - hence the 'scrawl' enclosed note that accompanies chapter 2. It includes dialogue from mum, I hope you enjoy it. I really haven't a great deal to say at the moment having spoken to you on the phone only the other day. Everyone up this end is very well. The only ones changing are Amelia and Adam - they keep growing bigger ??

See you very soon dad,

our fondest love, Garry and Jenny

X

SHAREAROOM HOTEL,

232,4534. ECHO DRIVE, RIVE, IVE, VE.

1st FLOOR PENTHOUSE,

CRICKLEWOOD,

LOS ANGELES, E.C.3.

CALIF.

DEAR HARRY,

SORRY, BUT I CANT REMEMBER WHETHER IT WAS HARRY OR GARRY OR BARRY, ITS SO LONG
SINCE I HEARD FROM YOU. AS YOU CAN SEE FROM THE ADDRESS, AT THE ~~MOMENTIXM~~
MOMENT I'M NOT IN THIS COUNTRY OR ANY OTHER COUNTRY FOR THAT MATTER.

I THINK YOUR BOOK IS COMING ALONG QUITE WELL AND SHOULD BE A BEST CELLAR...
FANCY ALL THOSE PEOPLE SAYING SUCH NICE THINGS ABOUT ME, AND IT'S FUNNY
REALLY THAT THEY SHOULD ALSO REMEBER THINGS THAT I HAD FORGOTTEN, NOT ONLY
HAD I FORGOTTEN THE THINGS THAT THEY REMEMBERED, BUT IN SOME CASES I'D
ALSO FORGOTTEN THE PEOPLE WHO'D HAD REMEMBERED THE THINGS THAT I HAD
FORGOTTEN.

HOWS YOUR LOVELY WIFE? PLEASE GIVE HER OUR (YOUR MUMS)
LOVE. STEVEN,) THANK GOD(SOON GOES BACK TO SCHOOL. I
HONESTLY THINK THAT EIGHT WEEKS IS SEVEN AND A HALF
WEEKS TO LONG FOR A SCHOOL HOLIDAY. HE SEEMS TO GET
BORED, BUT, I HASTEN TO ADD HE DOSE'NT WANT TO
OCCUPY HIS MIND WITH TRYING TO LEARN THINGS. HOW-
EVER YOU WERE THE SAME. MUM IS EXREMLY WELL.
~~XXX~~ AND SO AM I, AND I'M THRILLED TO SAY
THAT THE OPTITION SAYS MY EYE'S ARE NOW
PERFECT AGAIN.

SEE YOU,

LOVE DAD.

49

3

At Home

I have a certain amount of regret at not having left home when I commenced working in London. Life was so comfortable and easy for me that the prospect of flat-hunting in town and then paying a heavy rent spoiled my earlier eagerness to leave the nest. My parents were too soft on me. My mother kept hinting that perhaps I should consider the possibilities of moving out, but whenever it approached the crunch she would come up with a suitable reason that prolonged my residence at home. When I questioned her on the subject she even pointed out that most sons lived at home until they were married. I was initially adamant in my decision to leave but latterly, weighing up the losses against the gains, indifferent about a move.

Dad would have been pleased to see me go out and fend for myself in the world, but never persisted in encouraging my departure. On reflection I believe that he enjoyed having me around as a 'chum'. My being at home meant he had someone with whom to have a drink, go shopping to the tobacconist in Harpenden, talk and watch sport, and other similar pastimes. Having a profession that is not nine-to-five meant on occasions that he had many hours in the day to fill as he pleased. By the time I had returned from London each day – and I *was* nine-to-five – he would often be feeling a bit restless and in need of a chat about anything, such as

London Management (for whom I worked) and what sort of day I had had.

This desire for company developed into a need to 'perform' while in the company of my friends. Often a handful of mates would be sitting in my bedroom watching television, or listening to records, or maybe just chatting, when there would come a little tap at the door.

'Come in,' I would say despondently, knowing it could only be Dad.

'Hi there!' he would say, with a broad grin on his face. 'Are you all right?' Sometimes I thought they were *his* friends. Then he would continue. 'I've got a few of my shows on tape downstairs. Do any of you want to come down and watch them?'

I always thought this was a little rude of him. Some of my friends I would not have seen for a long time, and I would very much have liked to spend some time talking to them. But there was no way they were going to refuse his invitation. It would have been very awkward for them to say, 'No thanks.' So down everyone would troop and we would all sit and watch his shows in the course of the evening. I have to admit, though, that they were very much enjoyed, even if these evenings were not as I planned.

A friend of mine who made several visits to our Harpenden home was Rowan Atkinson, of late better known for his membership of the 'Not the Nine O'Clock News' team. One of these visits we spent sitting in the lounge with my parents and it was interesting to observe Dad giving Rowan advice. The mature voice of sound experience and success was giving incentive and drive to a youthful newcomer. Rowan was uncertain of his future at this stage. He was not convinced that the world of entertainment was in fact where he wanted to find himself. After all, he had studied and succeeded in engineering to a very high level. I can remember Dad saying to him,

51

'You must give comedy a go. You've got youth on your side. Just think how disappointed you would feel if, at fifty years of age, you look back at the comedians of *your* time and know damn well you could have been better. Frustration alone would be enough to kill you!' Rowan was, and still is, no fool. He is a reserved, level-headed man who listens to all advice that is given to him, and then deciphers it and produces his own decisions. Not once did he say to Dad, 'Yes, you are absolutely right,' nor did he disagree with him. I know that both Dad and I look upon him as being one of the country's biggest prospects, so thank God he did have a go at the entertainment world.

Although the occasional visitors storm the house, Dad spent much of his free time alone, just pottering around or playing in the garden. If a visit from a family friend coincides with a particularly restless period of his day, he usually gets up to mischief in the background. Only last summer, while

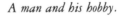

A man and his hobby.

the family was busy swimming in the pool, he suddenly appeared with a tripod and video camera, and dressed in the manner of a 1940s film producer – peaked cap, white plus-fours and a checked shirt. He kept testing the light so as to look very professional, and was totally immersed in what he was doing. When we had clambered out of the pool and changed into some dry clothes, he beckoned us to the sitting-room. 'Sit down and I'll show you what I've filmed,' he announced. It is always embarrassing when you watch yourself on a screen when there are other people in the room. Unfortunately these videos have sound, and so all the squeaks and comments we had been making were picked up. But in all fairness to him, it was a very cleverly put together little film. Despite the mundane choice of subject, we all enjoyed watching it very much.

His home interests are basically his hobbies, which include following the football scene. I asked him how involved he thought he was with football: 'Firstly, I must confess that I am not happy with all the problems now created for the game. I would watch and probably enjoy any level of game on television, but I don't go to *any* of the away matches with Luton any more. Luton are still my favourite team, though, because that is where it all started. I still have great affection for Preston North End and Blackpool because of the significance of my northern connections. But whatever division they may find themselves in, Luton will always be the number one for me.'

His involvement in the club started in 1968. It built slowly, reaching a high point when he became one of the directors, and then gradually completed the cycle with him retiring from his seat on the board and returning to his favourite position with the club – as a fan. Actually he became a fan 'with honours', as they made him a vice-president, which in real terms assures him of two comfortable

Luton reserves. Dad and me.

seats in the directors' box, with none of the associated hassles he had when a director.

It was on a cold winter's evening in 1968 that Dad decided to take me to my first football match. It was a toss up between Luton or Watford, but when we discovered that Watford were playing away that day, the choice became limited. Luton versus Oldham Athletic was the game we sat through. Although I have long since forgotten the exact score, I seem to remember that Luton put four goals in that day, and came out the victors. We were both smitten by the game, the atmosphere and the team. They were lowly and struggling, and we grew fond of their intimacy and the fact that we could be getting involved with a side of the future. (They were promoted to Division One in 1974, but were relegated the following year, but have just been promoted again.)

Although he was, and still is, no great businessman, Dad was the ideal man for the position of director. It was the chairman who realized that through my father's face he could promote the name and recognition of Luton Town. This is precisely what he endeavoured to do, especially using the Morecambe and Wise Shows as his medium. In his own words, he literally 'put Luton on the map'. No other director has or probably will manage to get Glenda Jackson to present a sign reading 'Luton Town FC' in front of some twenty million viewers. As a result, Morecambe and Wise have become linked with Luton Town in daily conversations. Even today at our Cambridgeshire hotels, I have heard football fans mention Luton and then move straight into Morecambe and Wise, or vice versa.

Whenever possible, Dad would support the away games and travel with the team by coach and train. In the early years he saw just about every home game, and if work interfered he would still have his chauffeur, Mike, keep him posted with match play reports I have even known him manage to tie up a live show somewhere up country with a Luton match played on the same day.

From 1968 until his resignation as a director in the mid-seventies he made many public appearances and put in a good deal of basic hard work for the club. His resignation was not caused by any feelings of dissatisfaction, but more because of a simple wish to be a fan again. He joined the club because of the enjoyment he found when experiencing live football, not for the financial worries and pressures that were to escalate during his period there. He had enough of those with his own profession. This is why he quite readily took the post of vice-president, which still gives him all the boardroom perks, but none of the headaches. And we both still love Luton.

Dad worked like a Trojan during the 1970s. It was the most demanding decade of his life, and so both home and family life were a little lacking during this period. Previously he had eased up due to health reasons, and now, in the 1980s, he is still recording and writing, but at a far more sensible pace. I do feel sorry for him on recollection of the seventies, when he was working so hard and spending such irregular hours at home. He had then and still has bouts of attempting to be domesticated − the true husband/father figure. Usually these efforts went painfully wrong, such as the time he decided to cook himself dinner. He and I were alone that evening when he announced that he was going to make us a meal. He asked me if I fancied something to eat, to which I replied, 'Yes, but not here, thanks.'

'Very funny,' he said sarcastically as he edged towards the kitchen, and began rummaging in the larder for the chip pan.

'Are you quite sure you know what you are doing?' I asked in a voice that held little faith in his culinary skills. I did not want to hurt his pride; it was not often that he attempted such daring feats as cooking. All the same, I did not relish the thought of undergoing a fatal experience as the price of a new thrill for him.

'Of course I do,' he said with a slight grin.

Well, he couldn't come to much harm playing around with a few chips, I thought, so I shouted, 'I'll leave you to it, then,' and moved smartly to the back door.

'Coward!' he yelled back.

'Enjoy your chips,' I said, 'I'm nipping out for ten minutes.' I heard him mumbling to himself as I headed for my car.

After being out for fifty minutes, a bit longer than I had anticipated, I swung the car in to the top of the drive and had not even reached the gates when the smell of burnt chips forced itself upon me. I hesitantly entered the kitchen, holding my nose and repeatedly blinking my smoke-filled eyes, as I felt carefully for familiar items of furniture I could cling to, so as to guide me to the opposite door. I made it across the kitchen and quickly opened and shut the door, leaving me safely in the hall on the other side. When my eyes had stopped running I looked for Dad. I found him in the sitting-room watching television, hunched over a plate of black chips, fork held dagger-like in his right hand.

'You can't eat those,' I said.

'Why not?' came the surprised reply. 'Nothing wrong with these chips.' He held one up between two fingers. 'Do you want to try one?' he said with a grin from ear to ear. He knew perfectly well that they were absolutely awful, but he was not going to admit it – ever.

'Not for me, thanks,' I said, nodding in the direction of the kitchen. 'What happened with the cooking? Have a few problems with the chips?'

He continued to put the burnt offerings into his mouth. I think he must have convinced himself that they were good. Had my mother presented him with a meal like that, he would have been furious. 'No, nothing went wrong,' he said, but without the grin. 'I had a slight problem when the chip pan caught fire, and I couldn't put it out. Actually, for a moment, I thought the whole kitchen was going up. But no problems.'

The smile returned as he crunched on the last of the coal-coloured chips, but that was the beginning and end of Dad, the galloping gourmet.

He has even made a few fatal attempts at gardening – that is, weeding and watering. One hot day he was restlessly pacing the house, wandering from room to room, looking for something to occupy himself with. My mother, in an attempt to get him out from under her feet, gave him a watering-can so he could water the flower bed beneath the kitchen window. She and I watched as he poured water on to the thirsty plant life. And then, as if to emphasize that once a comedian always a comedian, the watering-can fell apart. He was soaked. 'What the bloody hell . . .' he exclaimed.

My mother smiled patiently and said, 'It's all right, dear. Just leave it.' Then she turned away and started to laugh. 'He was trying so hard,' she whispered across to me. 'It could only happen to your father.'

'I'm soaked!' he moaned as he came in from outside. 'Can't you get one that doesn't break when you use it?'

My mother, still giggling, shrugged her shoulders. She had used the same watering-can for years and it always worked perfectly. 'Just a bit of unfortunate timing, dear,' she squeaked as, with dignity, but still dripping, he left the room.

I have already said that Dad is a secretive person. He loves to buy things, and, unless accompanied, he tells no one, especially my mother. Sometimes I would go with him on his strolls across the park to Harpenden. Usually the first call is to the tobacconist. He would generally have something specific in mind that he felt he just had to buy. I think money burns a hole in his pocket. The man behind the counter would produce a range of pipes and Dad would usually choose one and order maybe another two. Then he would proceed to the range of tobaccos, and fifteen minutes later, having settled on a new blend, it was the turn of the cigars. He enjoys Havana cigars immensely, but has always found difficulty in deciding if smoking them justifies the cost. Most of his Havana cigars are imitation, from a lesser quality crop. He says the difference in quality is minimal but the difference in price is considerable. He dislikes seeing me smoking a cheap cigar. 'You're not smoking that rubbish?' he says in a disapproving tone. 'You should smoke these,' he continues, holding up one of his better-range cigars. I agree with him, and when I'm a superstar too, I probably will.

After the tobacconist we either do a bit of general window-shopping or go to a clothes shop. He will see a tee-shirt or a jacket that he will temporarily fall in love with. With few exceptions, you can guarantee that, once bought, they are hardly worn from then on. Very occasionally after such an expedition, we take a short-cut home which passes our local pub. We rarely pop in there for a drink, as Dad finds it hard to relax with all the

Dad and Tracey enjoying a couple of good cigars.

people round him again. He does take my mother there quite often for lunch, however. He enjoys doing that as then he is not confined by the bar.

Looking back, I have very fond memories of our strolls across the park and fields, whether out for pleasure or purpose. Even up to the last weeks of my living at home, the two of us – and sometimes three, when Stevie joined us – would often spend the dying hours of summer's evenings walking and bird-watching. Initially Dad would take along several bird-watching books, but over the years he has grown accustomed to the types of birds we would come across on our pleasantly repetitive strolls. However, if anything slightly unusual appeared, we would try our best to remember its plumage and colourings, and turn through the pages together on our arrival at home.

Equally as enjoyable as those long walks, that gave way to long conversations, were the hours spent sitting on the patio next to the pond. Many an hour have we spent watching the fish lethargically moving in the silent water. He has a name for just about all the large ones, including 'Jaws' for the big grey one with ideas above its station.

Dad is always more relaxed when he is away from the studios, and in this mood he is far better at coping with the bizarre claims people make about him. For example, one half-term when I was still quite young, my parents took Gail and me to a film that had just then been released, called 'Oliver'. We saw it, enjoyed it, and began heading back to our car, when in the distance I spotted the GPO tower standing proudly above the surrounding streets and alleys. I pleaded with my parents to take us there for dinner, but my demands were turned down. They did agree however to let me have a look at closer quarters. For them it was a fatal mistake. No sooner had we reached the entrance when my father was recognized by one of the management and before we were totally aware of what was going on, we had been whisked into a lift and urged into the restaurant. The meal was averagely pleasant, and the novelty of eating while completing a circle was most exciting. Dad kept us waiting in the lobby area before we left, so he could visit the gents. As he stood placidly at the urinals, gazing vaguely into the depths of the white tiles, he was joined by another diner. As he lowered his zip he gave my Dad a nudge. 'Have you seen who's in there?' he said.

'No,' Dad replied, inwardly anticipating what was coming next.

'It's him, Eric . . . whatshisname with the glasses.'

'Really?'

'Yeah! I've just had a long chat with him. He asked me if I wanted to join him at his table, but I told him I had to go now. You know how it is.'

Dad refrained from answering and left as quickly as possible. But it is amazing how often this happens to him. People make all sorts of claims of having talked and drunk with him. For example, a similar situation arose when we were on the QE2 later that same year. Two middle-aged gentlemen a little the worse for wear were draped messily across one of the many bars on board. Dad quietly sat down beside them and asked the barman for a scotch. As his drink arrived he could not help but overhear the conversation they were having.

First man: 'I've seen him, you know.'

Second man: 'Who's that you've seen, then?'

First man: 'Eric Wise, the one with the glasses and bald head.'

Second man: 'Oh aye!' (Longish pause.) 'Did he say owt to you?'

First man: 'Oh aye! Said he couldn't stop and talk for long. He was looking for his little fat friend with the hairy legs. That's what he told me.'

Dad downed his drink and made to take his exit. He

smiled politely at the two of them, allowing plenty of time for them to recognize him, and then bade farewell to two long and gaping faces.

This incident should be considered as a compliment in comparison to what can be, and once was, said to him when he was opening a fête, shortly after returning from the cruise. He had been joking with a gathering crowd and was just about to climb down from the platform when he was approached by a stocky little man, saying, 'I didn't think you were very funny, and I don't like your shows either.'

These sorts of moments are always very awkward for him (and for anybody else) to handle without becoming too involved, but Dad turned to him and said, 'That's quite all right. Everyone is entitled to his own opinion. And in any case, I only came here for a couple of laughs, and you're both of them.' Then he did a quick disappearing trick.

To a certain degree he finds these situations comical, but not so much as when he finds himself part of an amusing situation which is created from its basic naturalism rather than his famous face. This can be best illustrated by a short story concerning a trip we made to Lancashire one week when I was on school holidays. We had initially intended spending our time with George and Sadie at their home, but due to the good weather, the plans were changed and we opted for a trip to the Lake District.

Sadie loved a long car journey, whatever the destination was to be. We travelled quite a distance and then a particularly quiet and attractive village caught our attention, so, after minor indecision, we pulled up for refreshment at its hotel. Tranquillity prevailed both outside and inside the building. We had little trouble in spotting a free table in the deserted dining-room and so comfortably arranged ourselves on the wooden seats. The silence of the room immediately created that dreadful feeling of nervous embarrassment, and so already a slight twinge of amusement was beginning to pull at the corner of Dad's mouth. 'We could have found somewhere a little quieter if we'd tried,' he said, trying to hold back his laughter.

'Ssh, the waitress is coming,' whispered Gail.

A woman in black dress and white apron approached and glared at us for a few minutes, then handed out some badly-stained menus.

'Thank you, young man,' said Dad as he opened his menu. Actually he did not open his menu. He pretended it was stuck together until she fetched him another.

'Do ya want anyfing to drink?' she then asked in an uninspired manner.

'A glass of water and six straws,' said Dad as quickly as he could manage.

We ordered our drinks, and then reordered our drinks as she discovered that she was unable to read back her own handwriting. It was when she made her way from our table to the kitchen for the third time that my mother made an interesting comment. All the floor boards creaked with such distinction you almost thought they were in some sort of pain. The total emptiness of the room produced an echo that amplified the sound out of all proportion. As the waitress returned she appeared to be making a conscious effort to disguise the noises by walking on tiptoe. Dad fell about.

The restaurant then began to fill up with business people out for a quick meal (not much chance of that), and other day trippers. The volume of sound now developed into such a crescendo under all these feet that it soon became obvious we would not be able to understand our own conversation against the competing floorboards. By now Dad was laughing painfully, and conversation anyway had become a thing of the past.

One other point that remains firmly embedded in my

mind, was the appearance of two old men outside the entrance to the hotel as we left. They had recognized Dad and one was saying to the other, 'Do you think that's his wife or his bit of stuff?'

I was about to approach them to let them know when George leaned a firm hand on my shoulder and shook his head. He was probably quite right to deter me. I will always remember that happening, yet it seems so silly looking back on it. I mean to say, as if he would take his wife to a place like that!

Probably the most awkward and amusing situation that I found myself in with my father was at a football match some years ago. Dickie Davies had invited us to a cold Wembley Stadium to see the qualifying match between England and Poland. We watched the game together but were separated from Dickie shortly after attempting to leave the stadium. However, we had previously arranged, should this occur, to meet up with him at a nearby hotel, where he was based for the night, so were not too worried. But the crowds were thick and strong and it became obvious that unless we pushed and shoved a little we would soon be taken off our feet by the surging waves of pressure.

Dad can be very decisive when he wants to be, and now was one of those times. 'Come on, Gary. We are going to cut across,' he said as he leaned to the right.

I was not as enthusiastic as he was about the direction change. It meant cutting across the paths of other, equally impatient people. Sure enough, one large woman was unamused by our attempts to free ourselves from the throng. 'Do you mind, mister? We're all trying to get outta here as well, yer know.'

'Sorry, madam,' said Dad as we continued our struggle. 'It was an accident. If you give us a kiss I'll prove it.' He was quoting one of his catch-phrases.

Whether her reaction was a result of the panic and fear of

being half-crushed, or whether it was because she was easily upset, I am unsure. All I know is that Dad's comments were all she needed to become really upset. She started throwing punches at him, much to the amusement of the other sardines. She succeeded in cutting his bottom lip and knocking his glasses off. We were both a little stunned.

'You just watch who you're talking to, mate,' she ranted. 'My husband will have words with you.'

He was a little, plump and totally inoffensive man, but his wife was stating a complaint to him and so he did his duty and approached Dad, keeping a safe distance as he came. By now the crowd was rapidly clearing. The little man stepped forward and said in a virtually inaudible voice, 'Be careful who you are talking to, mate.'

'I'm very sorry,' said Dad, genuinely, as he replaced his fallen glasses.

What seemed particularly odd was that no one apparently recognized him throughout the whole incident. I suppose this gave him a sense of vulnerability for the first time in many years. However Dickie Davies thought the story quite hilarious when we met up with him again at his hotel.

Many of Dad's free hours have in fact been spent in Dickie's company and he and his wife Liz are frequent visitors to Harpenden. Dickie and Dad first encountered each other at various functions, but had never spent any length of time in each other's company until their paths crossed in Portugal, when the Davieses were staying at Muriel Young's villa, just opposite from ours. 'To me he is the biggest star in the country and so I will have to admit that on our first real get-together I was in awe of the man,' says Dickie. 'This made it very difficult, at least from my point of view, to create a relationship between us for a fair period.' But eventually a marvellous friendship did blossom between them and has continued to do so even though their separate lives are extremely hectic.

Dickie recalled to me one of the earlier times when we met up on that holiday. 'I remember when our two families merged together for a day. Your brother Stevie was very young, no older than five, and had a wonderfully colourful vocabulary with an extensive use of swear-words. I believe Eric was rather embarrassed at times by his young son's raw character. On hearing him swear, Eric would turn to your Mum and say, "Oh Joan, tell him. He mustn't get away with it." The responsibility of handling him and disciplining him was of course Joan's, not Eric's. Having seen me on television as Dickie Davies, there was no way that Stevie was going to refer to me as Mr Davies. I simply became Dickie. Eric and I were standing by the pool and Stevie was paddling in the shallow end – up to his neck – when he suddenly shouted out, "It's f—ing cold in here, Dickie." Inwardly this made me fall about laughing, having not expected it from a five-year-old. He was a wonderful little boy, though, whom I grew immensely fond of, and I was so glad that I was able to assist in his learning to swim that holiday.'

We all met up again in Portugal the following year. There were quite a few of us, as both families had brought friends with them. We went to a restaurant in Albufeira one evening, and as we left we decided it would be nice to have an ice-cream as the restaurant did not serve 'puddings'. Dickie continues the story: 'Your mother organized the purchasing and passing out of these ice-creams and we all sat down at a terraced café to eat them. Despite the twelve or more ice-creams she had bought, she managed to overlook Eric. He kept mumbling on all the time we ate ours, almost making us feel guilty. "Marvellous," he said, with a look of sadness on his face. "I bring everyone out here on holiday, I'm the head of the family, and I'm the one who gets forgotten about."

'The ice-creams were inside paper cups and as the first

Dickie Davies teaches Stevie to swim.

of us finished I remember him picking up the cup and doing his full Schnozzle Durante bit – "Sittin' at my piano the other day . . ." What impressed me was that suddenly he was an international comedian, because of this visual act he was putting over. The local people were hysterical as they thronged around him doing this ad-lib performance.'

Dad has never had much patience with children. Because of this I asked Dickie how his two children, who were then in their early teens, got along with my father.

'Firstly, Eric was very tolerant with them, probably because they were not his own, and his attitude indicated that he wanted them to forget he was a star. He didn't want that image to remain among friends. He treated the boys on a man-to-man basis. This made them want to act grown-up, and so they didn't feel like misbehaving when in his company which I think was a very good thing. He could be quite critical of them, but in the nicest way. Both my sons, Dan and Peter, wrote the piece of music and accompanying lyrics that appear in Eric's novel *Mr Lonely*. On receiving it Eric said, "I like the melody. Take it back and work on it, and if it's any good I'll use it." And so he actually commissioned them in the end to write this piece in his book.'

The first time that Dad went to stay with Dickie was in the latter part of the seventies. Dickie had arranged two days' fishing on the Test for him, although he himself was not a fisherman. 'He was like an excited child awaiting Christmas morning,' Dickie remembers, 'because the Test is one of the best trout streams in the country. Perhaps that weekend was the first time I was totally relaxed with him, and saw Eric purely as a good friend rather than the legendary name that he is.

'His excitement about fishing on the Test must have made him a little over-anxious because he began to snatch at the fish rather than play them out thoughtfully. Mickey Lunn was the bailiff on this stretch of water and was slightly worried by Eric's performance. Consequently he literally took him to one side and had a quiet word with him. But after the talking-to, your father pointed out to him that he was simply nervous being on such an important piece of water and asked how Mickey would feel if he were invited on the Morecambe and Wise Show, to stand in front of twenty million viewers. Mickey understood this and left Eric to get on with it. As a result he relaxed and went on to have a particularly successful day, catching four marvellous trout in all. I was unable to watch him that day, so I drove home in the evening to be greeted by a proud Eric who couldn't wait to show me his catch. Liz was unable to put anything in her 'fridge as Eric had taken up each shelf with one of his fish.

'I accompanied him the next day to the river, just to observe. This was quite revealing to me as I saw that Eric

A good day's fishing.

possessed a very serious side to his nature, when out fishing. I knew nothing about fishing, so Eric enjoyed explaining a few basics to me, as well as ushering me around as he seemed to feel that I was in the way all the time. "This is a serious business, Dickie. I don't want you messing around," he said, which was a lovely anachronism as I had always considered *him* to be the one likely to be messing around.'

Having my father to stay only weeks before his heart operation was a particularly emotional experience for Dickie. 'There was a man who was obviously going into a very serious operation, though one that has now become almost commonplace. At that time he was very ill, and quite honestly not likely to have lived for any length of time. Naturally he was apprehensive, even afraid of what the outcome was going to be. That weekend we burned the midnight oil quite freely, just making idle conversation to help keep his mind off things. Basically he didn't want to be alone. Staying up late, talking, helped diminish the night. "It's no good going to bed," he said, "I won't sleep."

'On the Friday night – in fact by then it was 3 am Saturday morning – I had to go to bed otherwise I would not have been able to cope with "World of Sport" that day. "I must have some sleep, Eric," I said as gently and affectionately as I could manage. "I have to leave at seven."

' "Oh, that's all right," he said quietly, "I'll be okay. You go ahead."

'Now you know what Eric can be like when he wants sympathy. The head drops and the eyes roll and he walks around the room with a pitiful stance. As I went to leave the room he said, "Well, it's me and the Valium, I suppose.'

'I did manage to overcome his efforts to detain me. I had to, were I to make the show that day.'

During his initial recovery period, Dickie visited Dad in Harpenden, and was saddened to see how down he was and how much pain he seemed to be in. He recalls, 'At first I just thought, "Well, I hope that the op has worked out." But then I realized these things need time, especially when you consider what physical trauma the body has to experience in an operation of this sort. Sure enough, each day brought him greater relief. His biggest enjoyment derived from showing me his scars. "The mark of Zorro is now upon me," he would say, happily exposing his chest.'

Dickie and my Dad have also worked together. Dad appeared on a Christmas edition of 'World of Sport', and although it was a slightly shorter version than normal, he stayed for the whole duration. Previous to this they had had lunch at the Savoy Grill with John Bromley (Head of Sport) to discuss the procedure for the show. The theme that they had created was that Dad had come to the 'World of Sport' Christmas party, but had arrived early – right at the start of the show, instead of after it. He was to march in holding a bottle of whisky as his contribution to the party, and this also acted as a useful prop for him. Throughout the show Dad was to keep asking Dickie, 'When's the party, then?' and Dickie was to keep responding, 'The party's after, Eric – you're too early.' Every link that Dickie was to do in the show Dad was to be a part of. Apparently, during the lunch, Dad virtually took over the arrangements for the show, as Dickie recalls. 'I think we were much more nervous about it than Eric, who in a totally relaxed manner explained to us how he felt his appearance should be carried out. "We're going to be working together for the first time," he stated. "Don't try and push the humour yourself, Dickie. I never push it. Just let it happen around you. You just be Dickie Davies of 'World of Sport', and I'll do all the things that will elicit the humour. And I promise you that you won't come out of it badly, because I won't send you up or take the mickey."

'I did as I was told, and with the agreed basic theme

running throughout the show, it was more than just a brilliant success. Eric totally ad-libbed for the whole two and a half hours. I discovered that if you *do* work with E. Morecambe Esquire, he *won't* let you come out of it badly, as long as you contribute to the humour as a straight man, and do not try to be the big personality yourself.'

Dickie Davies and my father also have a mutual friend in the legendary Cary Grant. This friendship materialized three years ago at the Royal Lancashire Hotel, where they were visiting the Fabergé Trade Fair. Dickie effected the meeting between Cary and Dad, and they had a meal together, a 'champagne campaign' dinner, as it was called. Cary Grant recalls the occasion: 'I will never forget that day. We spent a wonderful lunchtime together, especially Eric and I because we went down vaudeville memory lane, remembering names of the past eras. It was an ideal topic for me, because I started out in vaudeville myself. I remember telling Eric that I had actually appeared on the same bill as George Formby, which rather puzzled him; but not as much as when I pointed out that I was referring to George Formby *Senior*, not his son.'

After they had finished their meal, Dad thought they should pay a visit to the men's room. Dickie felt almost like an outsider as Cary and Dad continued to reminisce about the old days. 'While we were in the toilets, a man came in, recognized your father and asked whatever happened to Wilson, Kepple and Betty,' remembers Cary. 'Eric replied, "Not a lot. Two of them died." And that just finished me off. I fell about laughing. I'm sure that Eric's reply was well established with the British public, but I had not heard it used like that before, and I will never forget it.'

And what of Dad's memories of Cary? 'As a young boy, I was always a big fan of Cary Grant's. It seems happily ironic that he is now also a fan of Morecambe and Wise.

His roots are in Bristol, and so although he lives in the States, he would come home once in a while to see his mother. Ernie and I were doing pantomime in Bristol many years ago, probably in the fifties, and it coincided with one of his irregular home visits. That was the first time we met, and then again in Bournemouth when he travelled down to see our show and spend a couple of days there resting. He never seems to grow any older. No doubt he will appear still charming, suave and ever-youthful when he is a 108.'

Dear Dad,

With the typewriter back to working order I enclose chapter 3
for your perusal.

I like this chapter as it shows more of the home-life than the
public-life, image.

Anyway, there is little to no news at present, so I'll leave it
with you,

Love to all,

GARY.

K.G.B. HEAD-
QUARTERS.
c/o R. REAGAN.

WASHINGTON.

NEWCASTLE ON CHESAPEAKE.

U.C.P.

DEAR GARY,   FIRST OF ALL LET ME SAY HOW UPSET I AM, NOT ABOUT

THE BOOK, BUT ABOUT THIS PAPER. I WENT INTO SMITHS AND ORDERED MY NORMAL TYPING

PAPER AND LOOK AT IT. ITS ALL OUT OF SHAPE. THINGS ARE NOT WHAT THEY USED TO BE.

I'm sorry But ill finish By thursday.
I shall take it back to Smiths.
This afterhoon. Good luck for the
future—
            Love
               Dad.
P.S.
   Liked the Poem. Give my
Love to Tracy.

75

4

At Work

My memories as a boy of watching my father at work at BBC
Television Centre, Shepherd's Bush, are very fond ones. As
I remember the numerous times during the late sixties and
early seventies when my friend Bill Drysdale and I dragged
ourselves along with him to the studios, I often think what
an irritant having two children to contend with while trying
to perform must have been. Much preparation went into
each of the shows, especially the Christmas ones. Bill and I
were very fortunate. No one was allowed to see the 'quicky'
sketches, and many of the dance routines were recorded on
a Saturday night, twenty four-hours before the audience
arrived to see the final product. Therefore we really *did* see
the creation of the Morecambe and Wise Shows. On the
Saturday there was no audience, just producers, technicians,
and the rest of the crew. We enjoyed this more than the
final performance and recordings that went on during the
Sunday evening. We felt very privileged, sitting there on
some important cable and filling our faces with sweets. Dad
was marvellous with the pair of us. As each section was
completed (which could take anything from half an hour to
three hours) he – and Ernie too – would fill in time awaiting
clearance from the producer's control room by joking around
with us. It was almost like a private show. Quite often the
cameramen would sit back and have a laugh with us. Those

recordings were my first experience of comedy without laughter. It is very strange, knowing that you want to laugh at a performance, but instructed to keep silent so that the microphones pick up no sound other than those of the artiste.

On the Sunday night, after all the recordings had been completed and the audience had begun to make their way home, guest stars and everyone else concerned would cram into one of the tiny dressing-rooms for what I suppose was called a party. Dad was more tensed up about these preparations than for the show itself. Perhaps that is not totally true, as it was the pressures caused by the show that brought out all his overreaction to the minor problems. For instance, arranging a dressing-room gathering with enough BBC mugs to go around became a major effort for him. If everything was not running one hundred per cent as planned – and it never does – he would blow a fuse, and my mother would have to smile and cover up his outburst with gentle conversation, almost willing everyone to believe that he was not really upset. At least his outbursts were short and sweet, and bad moments were soon forgotten. The Morecambes, short of the night porter, would always have to be the last to leave. My mother could never comprehend why we would always have to stay on so late. Ernie and Doreen managed to leave at a far more reasonable hour. Dad's excuse was that as host of the evening it was the correct procedure for him to stay until the death. But it also meant a relatively heavy drinking session. Sometimes he would weave his way out of the dressing-room the worst for wear and my mother and our driver, Mike, would have to help him into the front seat of the car. I could not criticize him for leaving the studios like this. All the tensions were lifted from his shoulders, so I can imagine it would be easy to celebrate more than one normally would.

The first ten minutes of the journey home would be like

'Twenty Questions'. 'How was the show? What did you think of such and such a sketch? I think Ernie worked really well tonight.' And then he would go silent as if someone had sneaked up from behind and coshed him. Really he was utterly exhausted. Falling into bed, he would remain in a deep sleep until the next morning, and all of that day he would be on edge until the tranquility of home allowed him to unwind.

His producer for many years on and off was Johnny Ammonds. He has lived and breathed the production of Morecambe and Wise Shows, and I asked him how it all came about.

'I was a sound-effects boy at the age of sixteen, so I've been in the trade for a good number of years. In fact, people I have worked with say that I have made the tea for Marconi, but that's not absolutely true. I was put on a radio series with Eric and Ernie called "You're Only Young Once" in Manchester, and that was the beginning of our relationship, circa 1954. They were fairly established as a double act on the radio by this time, having already done other series with different producers.

'In many ways, as a team, we were pioneering in creating Morecambe and Wise on the radio. It was an exciting time for us. Other names were up and coming too, such as Harry Worth, who was one of the first people I worked with on radio in Manchester.'

Dad, Ernie and Johnny would assemble at Broadcasting House, Piccadilly, Manchester and they would peruse scripts supplied by a man called Frank Roscoe. As Johnny recalls, 'Eric and Ernie would bring their gag books with them and each show was virtually put together on the Sunday. Speed was essential. Guests would include Harry Secombe, Derek Guyler and Hattie Jacques.'

It was during their association with Johnny in Manchester that they went to London to do the ill-fated 'Running Wild' television series. 'They had none of the people on the television series who had been working with them on the radio series, so it was a strange set-up for them,' remembers Johnny. After that they continued to do more radio series for a year or two.

Johnny went over to full time television in Manchester in 1958, and the next time he saw Dad and Ernie was in the early sixties when they joined ATV for the first of many successful television series. He was not working with them, but they renewed their friendship. As Johnny said, 'I was with the BBC, and didn't produce the boys until they moved to the Beeb in the late sixties. Bill Cotton came up to me one day and said, "How would you like to produce Morecambe and Wise?'

'I thought he was kidding. "They're with ATV, so there's no chance of that," I said. He went on to tell me he had pulled them over from ATV to the BBC.'

Johnny was producing Val Doonican at that time, and had been for three years. He had to come off the show to take on work with Dad and Ernie. 'I gather Eric and Ernie specifically requested that I produce their show, having worked with them on the radio shows all that time back. Working with them then was very different from today. We were given three weeks to put the shows on, and that included the design and scenery work to be sorted out. The first series was a big success and then, to shock us all, completely out of the blue, Eric had his first heart attack while working cabaret in Leeds. He wrote me a letter while he was recovering in hospital, in response to one from me, wishing him a speedy recovery. It read:

Dear John,

Thanks for your letter. I must say I am feeling a lot better now, although I am told that it was a very near thing – but as I told the doc, I have always had a near thing.

If I had got to the hospital half an hour later, it would have been the '— and Wise Show'. When they rang home, Joan was told that I had a ten per cent chance of pulling through – which Billy Marsh [Eric's agent] took!

However, things are good now, and if I take it easy, in fifteen years' time I should be back – *in here* that is! Three months from now I have been told I can ease myself in again. Thank Hattie [my assistant who had sorted out some of the problems incurred through Eric's illness] and give my love to Wyn [my wife].

That's all for now, except to say that while I have been here I have had over one thousand letters and one hundred telegrams which, if you work it out, gives me a RI of 84. [This is a reference to television reaction index, which is a collated list of numbers producing a viewing audience figure.]

The first Christmas after Dad had recovered and returned to work, on the night of recording the show, he went down with 'flu. Johnny takes up the story. 'He had turned up to dress rehearsal dosed up to the eyeballs with medicines, but was just too ill to perform. We had to cheat a little by actually filming some of the dress rehearsal, a thing rarely done, and added material from ensuing shows which was already in the can. I cannibalized these shows and knitted it all together and we had ourselves a Christmas special. Until now the public at large did not know. When it came to the invited audience watching the recording, only Ernie was there to apologize and explain what had happened. They seemed contented enough with the musical numbers and extracts, but obviously it must have been a big disappointment not having them both there performing.'

The success achieved during the following decade is common knowledge. The first series after Dad's return to health was also significant for the introduction of a new scriptwriter, namely Eddie Braben. 'That was the start of the quartet, Eric, Ernie, Eddie and myself,' says Johnny. Eddie had been working with Ken Dodd, and so was not unaccustomed to the bigger stars. Johnny stayed producing the Morecambe and Wise Shows until 1974. But as he explains, the time came for change: 'I felt that some of the ideas were beginning to be strained and that maybe other writers should have been called in. Eric and Ernie stated that they were quite satisfied as things stood. The outcome was that I decided to produce Mike Yarwood. There were no hard feelings between us; we would have never succeeded with hard feelings standing between us. In hindsight I confess to having been quite wrong in my views on the material. Not only did Eddie go on to do several wonderful series and Christmas shows with Eric and Ernie, but other writers and their respective material was not right for the boys. Ernest Maxim took over production as I did not work with Eric and Ernie until we re-joined at Thames.

'We have always shared an open relationship which I think has contributed to their success. Not only are we sweet and nice to each other when we want to be, but we also have rows. There was no way that I was going to say "Yes" all the time, as I know that would have been the last thing Eric would have wanted and expected.'

Shortly after their regrouping at Thames, Johnny went to visit my father at Harpenden to discuss forthcoming shows. Dad told Johnny, 'It will be good having you back because you will check me a bit.'

I asked Johnny what nightmares, other than coping with the time limit imposed, were involved in the recording. 'Fortunately the recording has always gone relatively smoothly,' he said. 'Sometimes so smoothly we have been worried that something must have been overlooked. It isn't right that it should go so well. But nothing will have gone wrong; it will simply be Eric and Ernie's brilliance on the night making it a fast and furious and above all successful occasion. Technical faults are the biggest drawbacks. We have held up the audience, and of course Eric and Ernie and other artistes, for over half an hour with sound problems and so on. That is very disheartening for them when they are trying to sparkle to a rapidly tiring audience. The most comical occurrences are supplied unwittingly by the props department. When Robert Hardy made his entrance into Eric and Ernie's flat, the door came away in his hand. When Terry Wogan made *his* entrance into the flat, one of the wall lights fell to the ground.'

As producer of Eric and Ernie's shows, I also wondered what members of the public say to him. He replied, 'People whom I know often come up to me when I am at home and ask if I can change them a bit. All I say is, 'Well, not easily, because they are what they are, as were Laurel and Hardy.' It is rare that a double act would want to change. I suppose the most repetitive question is, "What are they *really* like to know?" I can only answer, "Extremely professional, punctual and friendly people." '

A recurring guest star on The Morecambe and Wise Show, especially during the sixties, was Hannah Gordon. I asked her if there was anything in particular she could remember from working with my father. She recalled, 'Out of all the times I have now worked with him I have one particular memory I will always treasure. It was on the first show that I was working with Morecambe and Wise. Eric asked me whom I had invited to come and watch the performance. Personally I don't normally like having friends around me when I am working for television, so I said that I did not know and hadn't given it much thought. But then circumstances so arranged themselves that an old school friend of mine and my brother decided to come after all, so later on I told Eric that my brother, his wife and a friend were coming to see the show. "Really! What are your friends' names?" he asked. I told him they were Richard, Barbara and Anne. "Well bring them around after the show for a drink in the dressing-room."

'In those days the BBC always crammed everyone into the stars' dressing-room for celebrations, and more than often it could be a bit of a struggle to reach the door – let alone the room. However at the end of the show we fought our way through and sheepishly waved an arm at your father who was busy handing out drinks from a boxed-in position in the corner of his room. As soon as he saw me he dropped everything and struggled across to greet me. He had asked me in the morning for my friends' names, but since that time he had obviously had much on his mind, not least the lines he had had to remember for the show. But straightaway he said, "Oh this must be Richard, now which is Barbara and which is Anne?" I know it is silly but I was so touched by that effort on his part that it still brings tears to my eyes.'

The next time they worked together was on a Christmas show, and Hannah sang the 'Windmills of my Mind' song while Dad and Ernie played the part of the windmill mechanics in the background. On another show with Hannah, Eric and Ernie were standing in front of the tabs holding their usual line of conversation, with Ernie being courteous and gentlemanly, almost grovelling to Hannah, the special guest star, and Dad being rude and totally oblivious of who the guest star was and why they were there. For the spot, Hannah was wearing a rather baggy-sleeved dress decorated with lace. The sleeves tied at the wrists, and the whole outfit was very presentable. Hannah takes up the story: 'There was one moment when Eric was insulting me so much that I was supposed to look at my watch and say, "Well, if I go now I will just be in time to catch my bus." Normally I always wear my watch, but because of the design of my dress I had taken it off in the dressing-room so as to make it possible to tie the sleeves. It was the first time ever

83

that I had not replaced it. When it dawned on me that it was not where it should be, I decided I must, as a true professional, cover up my bare wrist with my other hand in a natural manner so that no one would notice anything. But Eric caught me disguising the absence of my watch and was not going to let me get away with it. Right in the middle of the spot he turned to me and said, "You haven't got your watch on, have you?" Then he spun round to the audience and continued, "She hasn't got her watch on, ladies and gentlemen. What an actress!"

'When you are on the legitimate side of the business you are always terribly proud to have covered up an error or whatever. The rules in comedy seemingly differ!'

One of the interesting points about Eric Morecambe, the professional comedian, must surely be his theory about why he makes people laugh. But his frank answer to that is that there is no theory behind comedy. Through trial and error over the years since the double act was formed, he had learned or discovered how to achieve a laugh and to continue to encourage laughter, without being able to analyse it. There are no solid reasons. Using his mass of experience, he is now able, as most professionals are, to glance through a script and know what will come over as being funny and what will be unsuitable. He can adapt himself to virtually any situation, and this is what is really being referred to when people say, 'He has talent,' or, 'He is gifted.'

Billy Marsh, the agent, has obviously played an important role in assisting Morecambe and Wise in their success, and I asked him how their breaking into television came about.

'Their first show was for the BBC and put on by the then Head of Live Entertainment, Ronnie Waldman. The show was far from successful, and it would be interesting to look back and see what it was all about. Unfortunately few recordings were kept in those days so there is no record of the show. Shortly after this I contacted Alec Fine who was the head booker for one of commercial television's pro-grammes. It appeared that I hit him at just the right time, for he managed to fit them into a weekday 'Star Time' spot. Eric and Ernie were thrilled and from this small and unsteady beginning they fell into 'Sunday Night at the Palladium', and made many guest appearances on other shows at this time.'

In an attempt to get them a series of their own, Billy rang Lew Grade one morning. Lord Grade's reaction might perhaps have been expected. 'You must be joking!' he said. 'I wouldn't give *them* a series.'

'Well, they are very good, aren't they?' said Billy.

'Maybe they are,' Lord Grade retorted, 'but they don't warrant a series of their own.'

That particular conversation came to a non-productive halt, but a few days later Lord Grade rang Billy Marsh back. What had made him change his mind no one knows, but Billy was not going to question his sudden interest. Grade wanted to know if Dad and Ernie were with either of the two current theatrical unions – Equity and the Variety Artistes Federation, which later merged. Billy replied that they were. Not surprisingly they had been with the VAF for some while. 'Okay then,' Lord Grade said, 'you've got yourself a series.'

It was Billy who reminded me of the time, in the mid-sixties, when my father was over in America doing the Ed Sullivan shows with Ernie. As a treat he decided it would be nice to take his Mum and Dad with them too – a prospect which thrilled George and Sadie. But Sadie was terrified at the thought of flying, so Dad arranged for them to cruise over on the *Queen Mary*, making sure they would be well looked after. 'And do you know, they were the only ones aboard ship who were not seasick during one of the worst crossings the *Queen Mary* ever made!' remembers Dad.

They arranged to meet up with George and Sadie in a

New York hotel on a certain day at a certain time, but the reception area of this hotel was enormous and I think my parents began to wonder if they would ever see my grandparents again. But right on time, there they were, George in his gabardine raincoat and 'Attaboy' hat worn at a jaunty angle, and Sadie, who only stood five foot one inch tall, wearing her best spring coat and white straw hat, and carrying a carrier bag. They looked as if they were back home, waiting for the bus to take them to Lancaster, shopping. It meant a great deal to my father, who had never before seen them so divorced from the context of their normal lives. I think it brought home to him what they were all about, and indeed what *he* is all about.

After a short while spent with my parents, George and Sadie decided it would be a good idea to see America by way of the luxury Greyhound buses. Having made up their minds, this is indeed what they did, and they had a fantastic time. When my parents met up with them again in England they proudly showed them all the photos they had taken during their tour. Unfortunately they did not have much knowledge of photography and each picture they produced depicted either Sadie or George standing in front of a brick wall, or gate, or door, which could have been taken in their back garden in Morecambe for all my parents knew. 'There you go, this one was taken in San Francisco, this one in New York . . .' and so George went on with virtually the same photograph of every visited place.

A subject which I know is close to Billy Marsh's heart is the beginning of the Royal shows which Dad and Ernie virtually started for him in 1972. Through my father's first serious illness he became involved with the British Heart Foundation. One of the gentlemen concerned with the BHF rang Billy after he had heard my father make a radio appeal on their behalf and asked if he could arrange for Morecambe and Wise to do a show or something for their concern. In an effort to produce something special Billy wanted to couple the show with royalty. The gentleman asked him which member of the family would be suitable for such an auspicious night. Billy's reply was that it would be wonderful to have the Queen Mother there. 'Well,' said the gentleman, 'I will be seeing her this evening, and I'll ask if she can attend. I will give you a ring in the morning.'

Somewhat to Billy's surprise, the man did ring back as promised. 'I saw the Queen Mother last night, and yes, she would be delighted to attend.' This was how Dad and Ernie and Billy became involved with the Royal shows.

Billy reflected on this occasion: 'I can recall on that night going into the Royal Box at the interval to be introduced to the Queen Mother. As she expressed her enjoyment of the first half of the show, which had included Kenneth McKellar, who was a firm favourite of hers, she asked, "When do Eric and Ernie come on?" The first-name terms momentarily stunned me, as I most surely expected her to refer to them as either the stars of the show or Morecambe and Wise. I told her that they would be on straight after the interval, but that I did not know the exact starting time, as they were making their way from the television studios. "Well, if you have to hold things up for a few minutes," she whispered gently, "could you possibly see that I am offered another glass of champagne?" '

I asked Billy to summarize his feelings about being involved with my father from a business aspect. 'The most wonderful working attribute of Morecambe and Wise is that they hold no class distinctions,' he said. 'Certain performers appeal to certain audiences; they have a style that communicates to one particular breed of person and so probably have a mass following within a minority. Eric and Ernie's approach to comedy is equally for the Royal family or for whoever can be termed the man in the street, and on top of that is suitable and enjoyed by children as young as seven or eight years. Your father is a very talented, privately introverted, professionally extroverted man, and, with Ernie, may the two of them long continue to bring us sunshine.'

It is a long time since I had my privileged seat watching Morecambe and Wise Shows in rehearsal. Christmas time is now the only occasion when I have any involvement in Dad's work, and that is merely as a critic. As with most families, Christmas is a very merry, festive season for us. We devour the turkey and mince pies, until we can swallow no more, and the drinks cupboard works overtime as the wine and brandy flow freely. Even the exclusive vintage port has its annual introduction to our gathering. The occasional disagreements are overlaid with brotherly love, as we happily sit round the table, stunned with peace and goodwill, to voice our jovial opinions above the resounding bangs of crackers. The presents are over, and after the mountain of plates and paper have been rummaged through and removed, we enter the significant stage in our family's Christmas. Like millions of family merry-makers throughout the country, we lounge back, relaxed and ready for the serving of humour that the television will bring us. I once read that the Morecambe and Wise Christmas Show is as traditional as Christmas pudding, and this is probably so. With our family gathering of close relations, we too huddle round the television set. For my Dad the relaxation, merry-making and idle chatter will temporarily die. For him it is the time to become the entertainer and star. Doubts enter his head: 'I hope the show's good – it seemed great when we recorded it. Perhaps the flat scene was a little long. I wish I was watching it alone, and could hear what the family had to say *after* the event.'

Whatever the public and press have commented, we have never been disappointed with a Christmas show. Dad is the first to say, 'It was good, but perhaps a little slow. I think that last year's was slightly better.' But we have not often been at variance during the passing of our judgment. As the show concludes the endless phone calls begin, bringing praise and comment, and we talk about it and talk about it, and then we forget about it, as we proceed with the rest of the night's entertainment. For Morecambe and Wise that is one special annual event which is over. In the new year it is back to the routine of the studios, and the hard work which they hope will succeed in bringing more laughter throughout the country.

Dear dad,

I'm sorry that W.H.S. could only supply crooked paper, if you have any more problems let me know and I'll lend you some of mine.

I believe you are aware of the problems my typewriter has been having — well it's nearly in working order again, hopefully in time for the next chapter.

Enclosed is Ch: 4. for your perusal — so far you have been very kind and considerate in your comments, is there any detailed points you would like to raise. If so please do, or forever hold our peaces.

I really want the book to be happy as, after all, that would be far nearer the truth than anything else — at least I was happy and still am and I know Gail and Steve were and are.

Anyway, leave it to you dad,

all fondest love,

Gary xo

CARELESS RAPTURE.

c/o. CAPTAIN BLOODLESS.

OLD SCOTLAND YARD.

OLD SCOTLAND.

DEAR GARY.

AS YOU CAN SEE I WENT TO SMITHS AND THEY REFUNDED MY MONEY, I THEN BOUGHT THE RIGHT TYPING PAPER. I THINK THEY THOUGHT I WAS A LITTLE CRAZY, ONE OF THEY ASSISTANTS TOLD ME WHAT I SHOULD DO WITH THE OLD PAPER, BUT AS I TRIED TO EXPLAIN , THE PAPER WAS THE WRONG SHAPE. HE LOOKED AT ME AS IF I HAD TWO HEADS. HOWEVER!

IVE BEEN LISTENING TO THE BUDGET. NOTHING EVER SEEMS TO COME DOWN, THE ONLY THING THAT SEEMS TO COME DOWN WITH ANY CERTENTY ARE MY Y. FRONTS.

RE. THE BOOK. DONT YOU THINK YOU'VE OVER DONE THE DRINKING? AFTER ALL IF I HAD HAVE DRUNK THE AMOUNT YOU SEEM TO THINK I HAVE, I WOULD NOW BE SITTING ON A PARK BENCH WONDERING WHERE I COULD GET MY NEXT GLASS OF METHS FROM. MY INTAKE AT THE MOST WAS HALF A BOTTLE OF RED WINE AND IN THE EVENINGS MAYBE TWO OR MAYBE THREE SCOTCHES. I SEEM TO BE DRUNK OR THROWING A TANTRUM IN EVERY CHAPTER. SAY SOMETHING PLEASANT ABOUT ME, YOU KNOW SOMETHING NICE, THERE MUST HAVE BEEN ONE DAY. THE POEM WAS GREAT.

LOVE.

P.S. THE NEXT TIME YOU HAVE A DRINK, REMEMBER I WAS STRONG ENOUGH TO GIVE IT UP.

5

On Holiday

As children, Gail and I were fortunate in having a successful father. In enabled us to enter a world of comfort at an early age, and holidays abroad were the first taste of good living that came our way. One afternoon early in 1963, my mother announced to us that we were going to Torremolinos for a fortnight. It must be said that such places were considered exclusive at this time, and had not yet developed into the huge tourist complexes they are today. Just to have our father constantly with us for such a length of time was a treat in itself, but actually to be leaving our own shores too made the occasion doubly exciting.

Like so many people, Dad on holiday is a completely different man. Most importantly he does manage to relax to a far greater extent than when he is at home. He also has time to observe situations and find humour in them, and also joke around much more than he would do in his own environment. When we were children he was quick to 'tick us off', but even quicker at making us laugh.

My memories of that first holiday in Spain are dim, but there is one event that remains in my mind, which occurred late one morning when we were lunching in one of the hotel's terraced restaurants. Dad had this irritating habit of removing the green stalk that protrudes from such vegetation as tomatoes, and gently placing it on the back of my hand.

This was supposed to scare me into thinking I had been visited by a cricket or some such insect. I had grown rather tired of this prank, and so took next to no notice of the insect-like appearance on my hand during that particular meal. It was when he clasped my arm so firmly, with eyes bulging, and lined his finger up to flick the thing off that I realized this time he was not joking. As his finger connected with the cricket it appeared that his watch had become loose. The motion of his hand took the watch from his wrist and it shot at great speed across the room, hitting a bald-headed resident at the next table straight between the eyes, before dropping heavily into the gentleman's consommé. The man was most understanding considering it looked like a deliberate attack by a mad Englishmen. Having rubbed at his sore head and with much deliberation produced a soggy watch from his lunch, he handed it back to an apologetic Dad who quickly replaced it on his wrist. 'There's nothing to worry about. It's waterproof!' was his parting comment as he returned to our table.

The hotel dining-room was a playground for his childish but highly enjoyable pranks. He could upset, surprise and bring laughter to staff and residents alike. Everything he did was in good taste as he would never want to feel that he had spoilt somebody else's evening. His favourite moment came when the wine waiter offered him a taste to approve. Dad's hand would purposely by-pass the filled glass and pick up the one next to it. 'Cheers,' he would say, putting the empty glass straight to his eye, missing out his mouth altogether. 'Sorry about that,' he would go on, pretending to taste from the empty glass. 'Oh yes! That's great. A little dry maybe, but great.'

Sometimes the waiters would laugh, other times they would watch in disbelief, convinced that this bespectacled Englishman had checked into the wrong institution. If there was a red napkin on the table his behaviour would deteriorate to an even greater extent. As the waiter brought the meal to his place he would grab a table knife, throw the red napkin to his neck and pretend to cut his throat, indicating that the napkin was a sudden gush of blood. Then he would collapse on to the table with his eyes wide open and glasses tilted to one side. My mother would smile and try to conceal her embarrassment. Gail and I would begin by laughing at him and then, as he continued in this way, start to kick him under the table and tell him to stop mucking around.

The following year we flew to the Canary Islands, which received a further dose of his antics. The holiday was only slightly marred by an event on our return flight. Looking casually through the window, Dad's eyes suddenly opened wide at the sight of flames from one of the engines, which, after a slight explosion, ultimately ceased to function altogether. Dad spent the whole of the flight talking louder and faster than usual to any of the crew who would listen, in an effort to persuade himself and us that there was nothing to worry about, and that we didn't really need that engine anyway. We did, however, land with fire engines roaring up the runway, which thankfully were not needed.

In 1965 we made our first visit to the Algarve in Southern Portugal. This proved to be the turning point in our holidays. I can still remember our first arrival at Faro airport quite distinctly. As we disembarked the sweet smell of mimosa wafted over the open expanses that lay between the aircraft and terminal buildings. The night was warm and sticky, and the air was as thick as honey. Continuing my parents' belief that everything they do in life is tinged with comedy, this trip exemplified their words. The hotel that we were to spend the fortnight at was owned by the Rank organization. Dad had been making a film with Rank just prior to the holiday, so they had contacted the hotel in advance and arranged for the assistant manager to collect us in person. They wanted to give us the 'red carpet' treatment.

On making contact with us he was to present my mother with a bouquet of flowers and accompany us to the hotel. Now, unfortunately for us, there was another family on the same flight that had the surname of Morgan. They had quite a surprise when the hotel manager mistook Morgan for Morecambe and rushed excitedly up to greet them. I imagine they were full of praise for Portuguese hospitality, especially when they were driven in a limousine to the hotel, having just been presented with a bouquet of flowers. We were left sitting in a now silent waiting-room while someone arranged a taxi for us. On arrival at the Solemar Hotel, we were greeted by a rather embarrassed assistant manager.

In spite of three days of torrential rain, and my customary holiday bout of tonsilitis, we had a marvellous fortnight. Among the people we met was a Portuguese gentleman who can best be described as an entrepreneur, and who was to play an active part in my parents' lives over the next five years. One of his many interests was in land, and my parents purchased a plot, along with the plans for a villa, from him, and eventually, and I mean eventually, a villa was constructed on the site. As well as the notably long time it took to be constructed, the villa presented other problems at an early stage, not the least of which was the sudden disappearance of the builder who had been given the contract. He absconded from the area with the money he had received for the job and was finally arrested and I believe imprisoned.

Our new Portuguese friend spoke good English and we soon realized that he fancied himself as a sort of Portuguese lord of the manor. One evening he held a dinner party for my parents at his home and was desperate to impress. His house is somewhat off the beaten track and it was only after some difficulty that they found it. He had often boasted of the many rooms he had, but failed to mention that each one was about seven foot square. The wife of this Portuguese gentleman could not speak any English so conversation stemmed only from him. Soup was served by a very strange-looking old woman, who had been made a waitress for this occasion, and who then hovered furtively near the door watching their every mouthful. 'She looked like Boris Karloff,' said Dad when recounting the episode to me recently. 'She had the physique of the Incredible Hulk, but twice as little personality.' She began to tug at Dad's unfinished bowl of soup, and he began resisting with equal force, unwilling to release his clasp until all the contents had been drained. She succeeded in pulling the bowl from his hands, and my mother's half-filled plate was also whisked away. 'I hadn't finished,' Dad whispered to my mother.

'Nor had I,' she whispered back to him.

Their host must have noticed what had happened. He leaped out of his seat and began rattling off sentences in speedy Portuguese at the maid. In time she returned the half-full bowls to my parents who smiled in embarrassment and continued to eat. 'But every time I glanced back, I could see one eye appear secretly from behind the dining-room door. It was as though she was spying on us,' said Dad.

As their meal continued their host repeatedly told them what a sympathetic man he was, and how kind and understanding he was to other people's problems and needs. 'As we finished our coffee he insisted on showing us the rest of his home,' continued Dad. 'We went into one small room where a tiny little mouse was scurrying across the floor. Our host literally went berserk. He started charging about, raving in Portuguese while attempting to kill the poor thing. Finally he trapped it and virtually kicked it to death. I shook my head in disbelief. Only five minutes previously he had informed us how kind and sympathetic he was. I wondered what he was like on a bad day!'

That first fortnight in Portugal was soon at its end, and so we prepared ourselves for the delay that seemed inevitable at Faro airport. This time we were kept waiting from 2.00 pm until 5.30 pm. The departure lounge was chaotic; nobody knew where they were supposed to be going, and the only functioning check-in desk had queues that curled their way round the outside of the building.

'Keep moving,' snapped my Dad.

'There's little point in moving if we don't know where we are moving to,' pointed out my mother while struggling with her passport, tickets and husband.

Just to add to the pandemonium, Dad was recognized by a fellow passenger who happened to be Cockney.

''Ere mate, are you in disguise?' he asked.

Dad replied in a similar voice, 'No mate! Are you?'

The man laughed before disappearing into the ocean of suntanned faces.

We were ushered into a waiting room to await the announcement of our flight. Our ticket numbers were something like BA 353 Faro to London. That was all very well, but the flight due to board just a few minutes before ours had a ticket number of BA 353A Faro to London. The difference was so insignificant that it passed unobserved and when our supposed flight had been called over the tannoy system we wandered out on to the tarmac with all the other desperate travellers. Relief came at last as the family slumped into the relative comfort of our adjoining seats. The steps were eventually removed from the plane's entrances and the engines were warmed up to a frantic pitch. The plane was all but ready to commence taxi-ing to the runway when a rather bright young air hostess noticed that there were more people than seats. She examined our tickets and pointed out the error to us, the culprits, who were taking up valuable space. She informed the captain of our error, who in turn contacted the control tower, and after a few moments the steps were brought back to the plane.

By now Dad had grown a little frustrated with it all.

'Come on,' he moaned. 'I told you it was the other flight we were on!' This was not quite true. As we stole down the length of the fuselage, trying to maintain our dignity, the passengers started to cheer and applaud us. They had recognized Dad and probably thought he had arranged the whole episode as a stunt. If only they could have seen behind the tight-lipped grin he had managed to summon up.

Shortly after stepping down to the familiar sights and smells of Faro airport, we were transported to the correct aircraft. To my Dad's delight, he discovered that his allotted seat was next to that of Tom Jones, and so had a most enjoyable journey home, immersed in conversation with the singing star.

However, despite the early building problems, happiness has always been maintained at our villa. After months of indecision we gave it a name, disregarding my Dad who wanted to call it 'Costa Fortuna'. Our first holiday in the

First visit to the completed villa.

finally-completed villa took place a couple of years later when I had reached the restless pre-teenage period that required the company of a good friend while on holiday. Consequently I dragged my best friend – and later best man – Bill Drysdale over to the Algarve with us. Bill and Dad have a good relationship, not least because Bill is the best audience he could possibly have, which encourages Dad to perform all the time. One morning at the villa Dad discovered Bill's incredible appetite, and in particular his ability to consume loaves of bread at an alarming rate. From that moment on Bill was known as 'Mr Wonderloaf', the name Dad has insisted on calling him ever since. He says of Bill's appetite that he has never met anyone before who can make sparks come off their knife and fork.

My father has a certain dislike for water. When he was a young man he was attempting a swimming lesson and nearly drowned. Now, if the water level, other than in his bath, should reach above his ankles he is taken over by instant panic. He also has a dislike for too much heat and sandy beaches. This means that his holiday activities are rather restricted. He therefore spends much time in the shade of a large sombrero, sitting on the patio smoking a long cigar and sipping a cool glass of shandy. In his hand he has a half-chewed biro with which he frantically scribbles down notes on a pad. Many ideas that were later to become major parts in the Morecambe and Wise Shows were conceived on that patio.

My mother describes Dad as being like a 'diego' when on holiday. He does allow his facial hair to spead freely over his tanned face, and his stomach expands rapidly over two weeks of easy living. I have always blamed his appearance on the hot weather. It could only be because of the sun that a relatively normal Englishman takes to prancing around on the patio in a string vest, a pair of black Marks and Spencer socks (he is scared of getting his feet burnt) and a tassled

Dad the writer. An idea is born.

sombrero that is four sizes too big for him. On numerous occasions he would approach me under his diego identity, saying, 'Son, one day dis vill all be yours!' As he spoke he would stick his finger out in the direction of the grapevines that lay at the bottom of our garden, and slowly and deliberately swing it around the horizon.

Our biggest enjoyment on holiday was to be taken out to dinner. Sometimes it was the case of a couple of sandwiches with half of the shore line spread upon them, eaten in a beach bar. But on the better times it would be a case of an *à la carte* meal in a small alcoved restaurant. Dad and I both love our food. We also love other people's company, but we both share the same bad habit of talking other people to death. It only takes one drink and then nobody can possibly get a word in edgeways. I think that we are living contradictions to the belief that it takes more than one person to hold a sensible conversation.

Cilla Black and her husband Bobbie were regular visitors

When in Portugal . . .

to the Algarve and we met them at Muriel Young's villa, where we had previously met Dickie Davies and his family. One night we all decided to visit a restaurant called La Cigale, and while our food was being grilled Bill and I listened to Cilla talking about the past and future, and her liking for boats and water-skiing. All the food at that particular restaurant was cooked on a large, open, charcoal grill and the smells that drifted across the tables more than whetted the appetite. During our first course our table was approached by a gin-soaked middle-aged woman. After throwing out some incoherent dialogue, she decided to fold herself untidily around my father. Dad dreads this sort of situation, but handles it very well. She appeared to have kept control over her blood-shot eyes for she recognized him almost immediately. 'I know who you are, young man!' she slurred. 'You're him. You're him.'

'If you want,' replied Dad, showing no embarrassment for himself, but a little for the company he was in.

'Oh. She's famous too!' she said, now focussing on Cilla.

'Yes, luv,' replied Cilla, trying to avoid her piercing eyes.

The woman's attention then fell on the glass that Dad was firmly holding on the table. Quickly, and surprisingly deftly, she snatched it from his grasp and proceeded to take a swig. At length she exclaimed, 'Ugh! What are you drinking?' to which Dad replied very quickly. 'That's very kind. I'll have a scotch and soda.' She laughed loudly at this but not for very long. The manager had spotted her and soon she was no longer entertaining us. Wherever my Dad may travel in this small world, no place, however remote, can guarantee him total peace and seclusion. Not that he has ever complained.

I have mentioned some of the people we have met at

Dad with the other son – Stevie, aged four-and-half.

Muriel Young's villa, but have said little of Mu herself. She is a producer for Granada Television, but I always remember her from earlier days on children's television when she was accompanied by two puppets, Ollie Beak the bird and Fred the dog. Mu is married to Cyril Coke, a television and film producer, and they own a rather grand-looking villa almost opposite to ours. Quite often they would entertain friends at their villa and one particular evening comes to mind when they were host to two German couples as well as the Morecambes. The Germans spoke English with superior precision and I can still visualize Dad as we left the party, fumbling in his pocket and producing a small coin which he placed in his eye as a monocle. With his shoulders drawn back and his chest barrelled outwards he grabbed my arm, saying, 'Tell me, Harry viz a G, vy you laf?' He paid little heed to the fact that we were not out of earshot. The Germans must have found us a trifle odd. 'Who is zis Englishman vizout a sense of humour?' he bellowed as I pushed him through the front door.

In more recent years Dad discovered other holiday resorts, notably Florida, which he now loves. Tracey and I spent a rapid eight-day trip there recently, joining Mum and Dad during their holiday. I will never forget our arrival at Miami international airport, seeing Dad standing there by the main door in a light-weight suit and with a straw hat on his head which I honestly believe remained there for the whole of our stay! Even in the torrential rainfall that soaked us at Disney World, he still insisted on wearing it – although he had on a waterproof poncho with a hood attached.

One morning he awoke very early in the apartment. I heard his door creaking open and presumed that he had risen early to start on his writing. Once his two uncoordinated typing fingers had started echoing endless tip-taps through the rooms and passages, I decided that I might as well climb from my slumber to see if I could actually catch

Waiting for the sun at Disney World.

him with his hat off. I could not! He was still in his green-striped pyjamas and dressing-gown, but the straw hat was already firmly in place.

Dear Dad,

And here we have chapter 5.

Firstly, I must agree with your comments that I have over exaggerated
and over emphaisised a darker side, and not followed through with
the happier times. I will re-think on that and try to balance it
more reasonably.

Chapter 5 is my favourite chapter as it covers the happiest times
of my life. It is amazing the memories that come back when reading
through this chapter. I can still picture you now standing on
the villa patio in your socks and sombreo, - marvellous memories.

Be hearing from you soon,

Love as always,

Gary

ERIC MORECAMBE,

c/o CHARLES HITLER,

BERLIN,

GERM.

DEAR GARY,

AT LAST YOUR MOTHER HAS READ THE **DRAUGHT** (ON THE WORD **DRAUGHT** I SEEM TO **PRESS**

THAT LITTLE BIT HARDER, ONLY ON THE WORD **DRAUGHT**, AMAZING) HOWEVER AS I

WAS A SAYING, YOUR MOTHER HAS READ THE **DRAUGHT** AND I THINK IS OF THE SAME OPINION

AS I AM THERE ARE ONE OR TWO THINGS THAT ARE THAT LITTLE BIT WRONG, THINGS LIKE

DATES, YOU SEE YOUR MOTHER HAS A REMARKABLE MEMORY FOR DATES, WE SEEM TO HAVE

THEM ALMOST EVERY DAY FOR 'AFTER'S' AND OFCOURSE SHE FEELS AND RIGHTLY SO, THAT

THERE'S THAT BIT TOO MUCH STRESS ON SUCH THINGS AS AN EXPLOSIVE TEMPER, SURE I

AGREE THAT I MAY BE A LITTLE ON THE PLAYFULLY LOUD SIDE BUT THATS THE WAY I AM

AND I HAVE TO SOMETIMES SHOUT AT YOU, BECAUSE, AND WE HAVE NEVER TOLD YOU THIS

BEFORE, BUT, YOU ARE DEAF. YOU NEVER KNEW THAT DID YOU? THATS WHY WHEN YOU WERE

A BABY WE HAD THE WORDS ' SPEAK UP ' TATTOOED ON YOUR BACK. YOU BECAME DEAF THRO.

SITTING IN A **DRAUGHT** .

WE TALKED IT OVER AND HAVE COME TO THE CONCLUSION THAT THERE

IS NO REASON TO REWRITE ODD PARTS, WE THINK YOU SHOULD REWRITE ALL OF IT.

MUCH LOVE.

P.S. YOUR MOTHER HAS JUST SHOUTED FROM THE KITCHEN. " GIVE HIM MY LOVE AND TELL HIM TO

KEEP OUT OF **DRAUGHTS**.

6

Illness

Illness has been the 'thorn in the flesh' of what has otherwise been a successful life for my father. Most members of the British public will have heard, even if they have forgotten the story, of Dad's first heart attack, of how he collapsed at the wheel of his car while travelling from a nightclub in Leeds. But while he was suffering in his way his family were suffering in their way too.

I was aged twelve when that first attack happened, and was attending a preparatory school in Hertfordshire, where I was a boarder. I remember having finished a heavy session of afternoon lessons that day and making my way back to the main school for dinner. As I was chatting with some mates and preparing to sit down at my usual place at the table, the portly shape of the headmaster appeared, pipe in mouth, to put a hand on my unsuspecting shoulder and silently march me into his office. Whether he thought I was too weak to take sudden shock, or whether he was too weak to give it, I suppose I will never know, but when we both stood opposite each other, he carefully explained to me that my father was suffering from a severe dose of 'flu. I really did not know what to think. His giving me a story like that in the privacy of his own office made matters worse, and I became convinced that something far more terrible had happened. I returned to my dinner feeling very confused.

The headmaster approached me again later that evening. This time it was to inform me that my sister was on the telephone and could I go and speak to her. 'Hello, Gary,' she said with no preamble. 'Everything's okay but Dad's been taken slightly ill. He's had a minor heart attack, probably brought on by all the work he's been doing this year.'

The bit about all the work he had been doing all that year flew over my head at the time. It is only now I realize what sort of pressure he was under, and also how badly he was treating his health. He told me he was smoking fifty to sixty cigarettes a day, 'and that's before I get to my own,' he would joke. He was doing live appearances at Batley while preparing material for two television shows, and was flitting backwards and forwards to New York to make television appearances with Ernie. They were also scheduled to appear in a show in Scotland for several weeks.

'He's in the Leeds Hospital and they say he's coming along fine,' Gail went on. In fact they did not think he would survive the night, and doctors had told my mother that she might not arrive in time, with the long journey to Leeds from Harpenden. They were hours of agony for her.

Somehow I managed to remain very calm. It must have been my detachment from the situation that made it easier for me. Poor Gail was all alone at home, my mother having set off for Leeds. Gail had the difficult task of ringing up all our relations – not easy for a fifteen-year-old. After an uneasy night, morning eventually arrived, and after breakfast I went to the school library where I found the school captain shuffling nervously, with the newspapers hugged closely to his chest. 'Sorry about your old man,' he said rather awkwardly. 'I mustn't let you see the papers today.' For one awful moment I imagined he knew something I did not. But then he added, 'I've looked through them, though, and he seems to be doing all right.'

I decided to go and see Mr Harris, a highly commendable

teacher, who was also a very awkward man to pin down. 'Come in,' he roared as I delicately tapped on his study door. 'Bartholomew, eh!' He rested his giant hands on his well proportioned hips. 'What can I do for you, boy?'

I swallowed nervously. 'Well, actually, I was wondering if there was any further news about my father?'

'Speak to you about it later, my boy,' he said, as he moved swiftly to the door and disappeared down the passageway. 'Your mother will ring you this morning,' echoed his fading voice. I slowly closed the door and went to my classroom.

Her phone call was greatly rewarding. She gave me all the necessary details and did not try to soften it up in any way. In the event, Dad got over the first major hurdle by surviving the first three days. Now it looked like a slow and careful recovery. Within three weeks he was back at home and as time ticked by the change in him was dramatic. He had become frustrated in the early stages, just stewing quietly with the inactivity. His greatest lift was when he conquered the staircase for the first time. This was followed by short regular walks around the garden with his favourite walking stick.

The major challenge came a few months later. Our local GP, Dr Price, came to give him one of his full check-ups. His reports were pleasing, showing signs of much improvement. 'Right then,' said the doctor, 'I think you're ready for a few holes of golf. Here, take my keys, you can drive.'

He threw the keys at my Dad who stared down at them in disbelief. 'Golf? Drive? But I'm ill.'

'Nonsense!' said the doctor. 'You couldn't be coming on any better. You're far too healthy to be loafing around the house with a long face and feeling sorry for yourself. A few gentle holes and some fresh air is just what you need.'

And so it was to be. Many games followed, right up until his full recovery had been made, and he was able to return to his partnership with Ernie.

It was over ten years later when his health failed him again. Morecambe and Wise were again heavily committed, with television work supplemented by live stage appearances up and down the country. In the late seventies they decided to move from the BBC to Thames Television, which brought about much publicity and controversy. Shortly afterwards, although totally unconnected, his health began to fail.

We as a family were very surprised when his minor blackouts and palpitations led to a second major heart attack. Stevie and I were having our breakfast as usual that morning before I took Stevie to catch his school bus, and myself off to the station. My mother was in bed with gastroenteritis and the doctor had made a call the previous evening to treat her. As always when there is a catastrophe, something else crops up to make the situation worse.

Dad decided to join Stevie and me that morning for breakfast, and we were in the adjoining room to the kitchen, about to bite into some toast when we heard a crash. Dad was on the floor, in front of the fridge, clutching the remains of a chicken.

'What happened?' he stammered as he attempted to climb back to his feet.

'You fainted', I replied as I helped lift him up. He was sweating profusely and resembled an athlete who had fallen from exhaustion three-quarters of the way through a marathon. His chest was pounding ferociously and his face was whiter than the thin layers of snow that almost coated the outside of our house.

'I think I'll be all right in a minute,' he said. 'Don't tell your mother.' The fact that he could be very ill did not initially occur to him.

I quickly packed Stevie off to school with the next-door neighbours and returned to help Dad move from the kitchen to the stairs, but he was unable to climb up them. He sat down on the nearest chair and huddled up as if he were cold.

He was beginning to look worse now, and it was obvious that even if he had just fainted, something far more serious was developing. He looked at me and smiled in a manner that said, 'Here we go again, why is it always me?' and said, 'I think you'd better call the doctor, Gary.' He shook his head, sending a spray of perspiration across the carpet, then he frowned and clasped his chest tighter. 'I can't slow my heart down. It's beating so fast.'

I rested an arm on his shoulder and leaned slightly forward. 'I'll call the doctor now. Don't move, just try and breathe slowly and regularly and keep calm.'

He chuckled painfully. 'I can't do much else.'

Seeing him in this state reminded me of the time when his mother died. Whereas his face was now contorted with physical pain, then it had been stricken with grief and emotional pain, and on both occasions his feelings were expressed through the creases on his face and the drooping of his head. The next few minutes went by very quickly. I had rung the surgery and suddenly there was a doctor taking Dad upstairs and examining him – a rather puzzled doctor who thought he had been called to see Mum. I did not have a clue as to where I should be or what I should do, so I slowly climbed the staircase and ambled into my parents' bedroom where Dad was now lying in a critical state, next to my mother who looked almost equally as ill. The sight of the two of them sprawled out in front of the doctor with two totally different complaints would have been comical had it not been so serious. I could read the frustration on my mother's face. She hates to be bedridden at the best of times, but with her husband lying with her in that state and her feeling too sick to move, the situation was quite agonizing.

'I must call the ambulance and rush you into St Albans Hospital,' said the doctor at length, before adding, 'if that's all right with you?'

Dad frowned even more and shook his head. 'If I'm very ill then of course it's all right with me.'

An ambulance arrived and he was carried into the vehicle on a stretcher.

'I think you had better follow us in your car,' the doctor said to me, moving to the ambulance himself.

'All right,' I replied, 'if you want me to.'

'It would be advisable,' he said in a low voice. 'His condition has progressively changed while I have been with him and I believe he has had a heart attack.' He was indicating that he could not guarantee a recovery and if he was dead on arrival at the hospital, as the most available next of kin, I should be present. I nodded and then the ambulance was gone, leaving a disturbing silence in its wake.

The St Albans Hospital is only a few miles away from where we live, and I was beginning to wish it was further away as I apprehensively pulled up in the car park. I had little trouble in locating Dad's ward but quite some difficulty in being allowed to see him. Eventually the doctor appeared and his expression was non-committal, which was probably best in such circumstances. 'He's awake,' he announced in a gentle tone.

'Should I see him?' I asked, not knowing the correct procedure, if there is one in such situations. I was taken through to the emergency ward and had literally to struggle to get anywhere near him. Nurses and other medical staff were working around him so busily that for a second I thought I was in a very well-produced American television cop series.

'Just a few seconds, that's all,' said the heart specialist whom I had met on several previous occasions at home.

Although pale, feeble and very ill, Dad's system had responded to the immediate treatment. He was no longer perspiring with such profusion and appeared therefore far more comfortable. 'Hello, son,' he said in a croaking voice. 'Not too well, am I?' He smiled slightly. 'Have they said how bad it is?'

'No. No, nothing, really.' I fumbled with my words. 'I think you just have to take it easy for a while,' I said, stating the obvious, but not wishing to alarm him more than he already was.

'Okay, that's all for now,' said someone.

I wandered out into the corridor with the doctor, who filled me in on all the medical jargon and described what exactly had happened. There was something very reassuring about his professionalism.

I went home and spent the day by the phone, handling the inevitable press calls and ringing round the family and close friends, in an attempt to assist my mother. The only enjoyable phone call that day was when national radio interviewed me for up-to-date information on Dad's condition. I felt terribly misplaced, having heard so many similar interviews and found them tedious and pointless, as mine now seemed. I could not focus on reality as the words left my mouth and felt embarrassed at my lack of information, to the point where I felt I should perhaps exaggerate to give them a worthwhile story!

Some days later I went to visit Dad in hospital. By now they had isolated him from the ward as he was no longer connected to the heart machine. 'Well done with the interview,' he said. 'You sounded very clear and intelligent.'

'I was very nervous,' I confessed. 'It felt so strange speaking about you to the public as though you were the president and I was your right-hand man.'

He shook his head slowly. 'Doesn't matter. As long as you speak slowly and clearly without too many umms and aahs, you can't go wrong.'

He was still in bed on this visit and visitors were not allowed to stay too long as they made him weak. By the time I next visited him he was far closer to his old self again. He was allowed to take short walks around his room and see people other than family. He asked me how my friend Bill was, and I told him that he was ill in bed with a bad cold. All he said was, 'Does he know?' He was as sharp as ever.

Soon he was allowed home. The weather was terrible, though picturesque, with inches of newly-fallen snow. He was put straight to bed with instructions to take things very easy and no excitement. Mum was doing all she could to make him comfortable. Alas, only a few hours later fate struck an unexpected blow. The house was very peaceful – I had gone to a friend's for dinner, leaving my parents to enjoy this first evening together, and there was nobody else at home. Dad settled down for the night while Mother took Barney, our dog, for a quick walk up the road before joining him. A few moments later she slipped on an icy path and fell. Some passers-by came to her aid and managed to get her home, where she dreaded the shock it was going to be to Dad. It was quite an achievement getting up the stairs and along to the bedroom to break the news of her injured ankle, which later on was to prove to have three fractures. It was not until the next morning that the ambulance came to take her to hospital for treatment. The same situation all over again – one in bed recovering and the other removed on a stretcher to the ambulance en route for St Albans Hospital!

Dad's recovery from the actual heart attack was successful, but it was later apparent that he would have to undergo open-heart surgery. The decision was simplified by the alternative of eighteen months of living and possible death any time thereafter. As he said himself, it was Hobson's choice. He was moved into Harefield Hospital and faced the most crucial hours of his life. Recovery for him, and many others with a similar condition who had the by-pass operation, was eventually complete. He was a little depressed during the early weeks of recovery but took it day by day as the relief from pain grew. I visited him at Harefield quite a while after the operation. I expected to see a very aged and subdued version of the father I had once had. I was pleasantly surprised. He was more concerned at finding a life-size plastic heart the surgeon had shown him when discussing the operation, than about my visit. 'What do you want it for?' I asked, not that I was intending to ask a duty nurse if Mr Morecambe could borrow a plastic heart.

'It's for when I leave the hospital in a few weeks' time. As I walk out the front door the press will surround me and ask questions while I'm being ushered into the car by your Mum. One of the press boys is bound to ask how the operation went, and at that point I will say, "It went very well, thanks," and then fall to the floor, holding up the heart and saying, "It's all gone wrong".' Luckily he talked himself out of this plan over the next two weeks of hospitalization.

During the last couple of years he seems to be fitter and healthier than I have known him to be for a very long time. He carries less weight and has given up drinking anything stronger than tea. He rarely mentions his illness and when he does he refers to it in such a calm manner you believe him to be discussing the condition of a distant acquaintance. And if you ask him if the scars still hurt him at all he replies, 'Only when I laugh.'

DEAR DAD,

ENCLOSED IS FURTHER MATERIAL. SORRY I HAVEN'T KEPT YOU TOTALLY
UP TO DATE WITH ITS PROGRESSION, BUT PERHAPS YOU WOULD RATHER READ
IT A LARGE SE CTION OF IT IN THIS MANNER ANYWAY.

LOOKING FORWARD TO ANY COMMENTS YOU MAY HAVE,
LOVE ALWAYS,

THAMES T.V.

SHEPHERDS BUSH,

C.T.V.

GRANADA,

YORKSHIRE.

DEAR GEE.,

I HAVE'NT MUCH TO SAY THIS WEEK.

WITH LOVE.

7

Friends

It is highly likely that a person who leads as hectic a life as my father will meet many sorts of people, but very few of these remain as close friends. My father is in fact a person who has found friendships with a range of different people from all kinds of backgrounds, and with all kinds of personalities. Inevitably, though, most of his friends come from the field of showbusiness, and some date back to the very early days in his career.

Roy Castle is one such showbiz friend, but he has more than just a professional connection with Dad. 'Many people probably won't know, but Eric was responsible for my marriage to Fiona, whom the Morecambe family had known long before I came on to the scene,' recalls Roy. 'Whenever Fiona and I row, I feel like throwing pebbles at Eric's window. The whole incident of my introduction to Fiona was typically Eric. It happened on a Sunday in July 1962, when Eric and Ernie were guesting on my show at the Wood Green Empire. Eric wandered into my dressing-room with a sly look on his face. "There's a young girl who would like to meet you, Roy," he said in a serious tone that straightaway spread doubt in my mind. "She's a great fan of yours and a good friend of the family, and I would like to bring her round to meet you." I began thinking that it was going to be one of those dreadful situations that Eric liked to put people in. I pictured some big, dumpy, giggling girl with braces on her teeth sitting in the corner of the room squeaking and pointing her podgy finger at me every few seconds. I thought that I might as well suffer whatever he had in store for me because if I didn't he would catch me some other time, some other way.

'"Yeah, sure," I said in a casual voice. "Why not?"

'Eric brought her into the dressing-room to meet me. And in came this lovely, fresh-looking girl with blonde hair, recently made-up for her part in the stage version of "The Sound of Music". In your father's inimitable style, he left her standing with me and as he went to leave the room said very quickly, "This is Fiona, and she's in love with you," and then he was gone.'

Part of Dad and Ernie's act in those days, was to do a ventriloquist routine with a life-size dummy, which gave him the inspiration to play a practical joke on the chorus girls. Roy was also in the show and takes up the story: 'Eric smuggled the dummy (how do you smuggle a life-size dummy anywhere?) down the corridors and into this single-seater toilet. He carefully placed it in a seated position with hands folded on its lap, and head slightly tilted downwards. A while later one of the girls made a visit to the toilet, and as she opened the unlocked door she was confronted by someone else apparently sitting there. On discovering the toilet was unexpectedly occupied she let out a short scream and backed out of the cubicle apologizing as she went. A few moments later the same thing happened with one of the other girls. She too let out a scream and quickly vanished. They approached Ernie and myself, telling us about this strange, immobile man who was in the toilet. We continued to play along with the gag for a while longer and then decided to tell them that it was just a prank set up by Eric, and all they had in fact seen in the toilet was the dummy from their act. At that moment Eric appeared and we all had a good laugh about it. The girls left the dressing-room and Eric without delay went straight to the toilet. He removed the dummy, hid it somewhere and promptly sat himself on the toilet with his hands folded and head tilted slightly downwards. He left the door ajar and waited. Sure enough, one of the girls returned and, on seeing Eric in there, leaped back, slightly startled, before thinking, 'Oh dear, they've forgotten to remove the dummy.' As she went to drag it out, Eric lifted his head and said, "Just one moment, madam. I have not finished!" The poor girl nearly died and it took a long time to calm her down.'

Some years ago Roy was appearing at a show in Coventry with Dad and Ernie and Arthur Askey and the singer Yana. My Dad, Roy and Arthur did a spoof routine in the show of the Wilson, Kepple and Betty sand dance. The two Arabs adorned in loin cloths and moustaches were my Dad and Roy. It was a very quick and difficult change for Dad to make as it followed straight on from his spot with Ernie. Previously the moustaches had proved to be a bit of a problem. Roy remembers: 'Eric didn't like the ones that clipped to the nose, as he was convinced that they would fall off. Consequently we used stick-on ones with added rubberized glue that we had found. "Here we are, Eric, you'll have no problems with this 'tache now," I had said to him earlier in the day.

'There is, incidentally, a dubious story connected with our 'taches which, for some reason, we referred to as "bowsers". The girls at the Windmill Theatre had to shave in a certain place before going on stage and the running joke was that they had to wear wigs for going out with the fellas, and these wigs we called bowsers.'

Anyway, back at the side of the stage, Ernie was trying to get Dad into his loin cloth and Roy was trying to stick this 'tache on his top lip. His face was so sweaty from just performing that it was not sticking down as well as planned.

Roy picks up the story: 'Your father wasn't very happy about the whole thing. "It's not staying on," he said angrily as the music signalling our entrance began. We fell on to the stage and commenced the routine. Our movements took us across the stage in one direction, nose to tail, and then we quickly spun round, the manoeuvre leaving me at the front, with Eric behind me, right at my ear. Suddenly, in a disguised voice, he said, "The bowser's gone!"

'It's the kind of comment that, if Eric made it anywhere, I would still have laughed, but to actually whisper it on stage . . . I was in hysterics. I didn't wear contact lenses at the time so my eyesight wasn't too hot, but as I glanced down to the floor for the next spin round, I could make out this black, out-of-focus furry mass – the fallen bowser. There were three of us from this show sharing the same hotel bedroom. Eric, my pianist and myself. We laughed solidly until three in the morning about the bowser, and then, overcome with exhaustion, we fell quiet. We dozed off for a few minutes, and then someone sniggered and that set us off for another hysterical laughter session. This went on virtually throughout the night. Every time we dozed, someone else would start giggling again.'

A further memory that Roy has of my father concerns the late tenor singer, David Hughes, and shows how friendship can conspire for its own ends. They were working at Torquay at the time. David Hughes was topping the bill, Dad and Ernie were second top, and Roy was third. Roy continues the story: 'The previous week to the opening of the show, David had done an Elvis Presley impersonation in his act, which had gone down a storm with the audience. The only problem was that he had to change into the right gear and this left a short pause, hence an empty stage. On that show he had asked the King Brothers to go out and sing a number until he was ready to burst out on to the stage as Elvis. Eric, Ernie and myself listened to David as he told us how well it had all worked out, and then he made the fatal mistake of asking the three of us to go out on the first night and fill in for him, in the same manner as the King Brothers had done. Eric looked at me and I looked at Ernie. Our first reaction was, "What a liberty," but Eric's expression could be deciphered to read, "You're treading in deep water here, sunshine."

'Whereas the King Brothers had filled in with a gentle little song, we three dashed on to the stage with our own routine worked out in a haphazard way. Eric turned out in a sombrero hat that was literally eight feet in diameter, a string vest and braces that supported a pair of short trousers. Ernie was equally gregariously dressed, and I was disguised as a tramp, complete with false beard and a coronet to represent the "busker" image. We more or less ended up by ad-libbing our way through our few minutes, not keeping to any format we had planned. The whole place fell about with hysterics. I don't think that our own individual spots had gone down as well as this seemed to be doing.

'David had by now appeared side-stage in his full Elvis gear, and was impatiently signalling to us that it was time to wind up and let him out there. "I'm ready, boys!" we kept hearing him shout in a dignified and restrained manner. We were having a ball out on stage, pretending to argue about what we were supposed to be doing. Eric grabbed the mike and started to sing, "There's just one place for me . . ." then he fumbled through his pockets and produced a crumpled piece of paper, and read, "Near you." He then replaced it in his pocket, Ernie and I took the backing vocals with, "That's the one place to be . . ." and then Eric would fumble in his pockets once more and produce the piece of paper and read, "Near you."

'This went on and on, and we had the theatre convulsed, while in the distance we could still hear, "I'm ready now, boys. Come off. I'm ready." Eventually, driven by total desperation, David leaped out on to the stage in his full Elvis gear with the Elvis stance, and the whole place that had just been filled with laughter went totally silent. The building had been transformed from a theatre to an enormous library with stalls. You could read the confused faces of the audience. "What's the matter with him?" they were saying. And, of course, he could not finish the routine. Eric began jokingly to push and shove us off the stage, while saying, "Come on, lads, we're not wanted here."

'We all shuffled off, leaving David there dying a death. After the show he came to our dressing-room. "I don't think we will do that routine again. I don't think it worked out," he said in all seriousness. I think a lesson had been learnt. Never let performers of the calibre of Eric and Ernie loose on to a stage with no set script or time-limit imposed.'

During the seventies, due to Dad forming a friendship with Graham Hill, he developed a liking for the world of Formula one racing cars. 'Yes, I suppose I did get involved with it in a very small way,' he recalls. 'I never became a fan as such, it was more that I was a friend of Graham's, and he invited me along to a couple of meetings. The first time that I went with him it was for the British Grand Prix at Brand's Hatch, and the second time was the British Grand Prix at Silverstone. Because of the bad traffic he would always insist that I go by helicopter.

'To me this was a totally different world. Helicopters and small aircraft were not the sort of things I was brought up on. I mean, I have always had a liking for biplanes. But I know I shall never get to fly one; I would be too frightened. It's that feeling that there is nowhere to hide if something happens. No—I had settled to go by car, although sometimes waiting several hours to come out of the car park at the end of the race left me thinking that perhaps I hadn't chosen the best way — even though I felt it was the safest.

'I think the most terrifying moment of my small

Graham Hill, a great friend, with Dad at Brand's Hatch.

involvement in the sport came when Jackie Stewart took me around the Silverstone circuit in a saloon car. It was something the *Daily Express* were sponsoring. On the straights we were going a hundred and twenty and God knows what speeds we were doing around those bends. Since Graham's tragic death some years ago, I really haven't been involved and I doubt that a reason for my involvement will come up again.'

Dad was requested to make a speech at Graham Hill's

Dad the speechmaker.

retiring party in November 1975. On discovering the notes
necessary for this speech tucked away under a mass of old
books and photos, I read them and decided that they were
so good I wanted to put the speech into the book. It reads
as follows:

'Your Royal Highness, my lords, distinguished guests and
gentlemen, how nice to hear so many wonderful things
being said about my dear friend, Gladys Mills . . . Graham
Hill. Graham Hill, the Arthur Askey of motor racing. And
how nice of the national sporting club to offer to go halves
on my dinner this evening.

'I shouldn't be speaking to you this evening, as I am
really the second choice. The man who was going to make

this speech unfortunately has been called away to the great eternal resting place. He has been given a permanent job at Chryslers. The food here [at the Café Royal] or, as it is called by the staff, the "chew and choke" . . . the food was, as always, mediocre. Not many people realize this, but this is still one of the few restaurants in London where you can get a five-course meal for under £2. Four baked beans and a serviette.

'A good speech depends on a good mike, and I am told . . . is . . . finest . . . mike . . . ever . . . invented. As I look along this table at what I can only describe as a middle-aged spread, I see so many of my friends, some of whom I have known for almost half an hour. And I say to myself, Ernie – oh yes, even I get mixed up. I say to myself that at this table there is not one fictitious character. Everyone at this table is either living or dead.

'We were going to have a surprise for Graham, we were going to cancel the whole evening and not tell him. We were also going to have a six-foot cake wheeled into the centre of the room, and a naked girl was going to pop out. When we took the cake out of the oven this afternoon she didn't look too good. So we scrubbed around that. She was going to stand there wearing only a pair of black shoes and black gloves and do a fantastic impression of the five of spades. And as she slowly turned around, she was also going to give the impression of a rather worried Kojak with a very deep frown.

'I am sorry to say that Ernie – you remember Ernie, the Bank of England with a wig – isn't with us tonight. This afternoon he met with a slight accident. He was cleaning Sir Lew Grade's car when his tongue ran dry. But tonight is for another man – your friend and his, Graham Hill. A man who, in one way or another, has been entertaining us for the past twenty years . . . whether we wanted him to or not.

'Who could forget what Graham has done for motor

racing? He packed it in for a start, and that to me is bad, almost as bad as having unbreakable Des O'Connor records. Who can forget the carefree image he created? The long flowing locks are still the same, because he never gets it cut. Every four weeks he has his ears lowered. Who could forget the now famous smile? Whether it is in victory or defeat, he is always smiling. He has to — as a kid he once swallowed a cucumber sideways. And who could forget that moustache? The last time I saw anything like that on a top lip, the whole herd had to be destroyed. And yet if you put all those things together — the hair, the ears, the mouth and the moustache, you have a face. And the last time I saw a face like that, Tarzan was feeding it bananas.

'Great racing drivers are like Graham's legs — few and far between. But then I could stand here all night saying these wonderful things about Graham. How many people here know that Graham — and I am sure he won't mind me telling you, and if he does, sod him — how many people know that for the past three years he has been studying in the evenings, studying to become a QC? Oh yes, Graham Hill is now a QC. Queer as a coot.

'You are probably saying to yourself, what do I know about motor racing. Well, I must be one of the few men in this garage tonight that have been around the circuit at Silverstone at a hundred and thirty miles per hour. I went around with my friend Jackie Stewart, isn't that right, Jackie? Jackie took me around at a hundred and thirty miles per hour for six laps. I can tell you this — it is a great laxative.

'You know, Graham is a very generous man. Only tonight I found myself short of money, and right away he said how much would I like; ten, twenty, fifty, one pound? He's all heart. Graham also likes to drink, like most of us, and why not, if he enjoys a drink. He once held up a ship launching for three hours. He wouldn't let go of the bottle. He is a complex man. A man who has his own car, his own plane, his own yacht, and still he walks in his sleep. He is a genius! The only man to make a U-turn in a car wash. To be a great racing driver you need three things. And if you have three things you should be in a circus. He is different from other men. He is the only man I know who fancies Hylda Baker. Graham is one of the élite. But don't think it has been easy. He has had to suffer. He has had to struggle. None of us will forget that terrible accident, but Graham, being the man he is, married her.

'It is not easy to stand up here and say some of these things, if you're not careful, you may end up looking a right James Hunt. But in a few moments Jackie Stewart will be saying some wonderful things, and what I would like to say for now is, Graham, every happiness and success, and thank you for your friendship. Thank you.'

In essence my parents have few really close friends in their neighbourhood. This is no fault of anyone's nor particularly viewed as a tragedy, as they have not tried especially hard to create close friendships, despite living in Hertfordshire for the past twenty years. As Dad comments, 'My line of business is so different from the norm that I have found it difficult to communicate convincingly with local people at parties and suchlike, and no doubt they have found the same problem with me. It sounds boring and conceited to say it, but I am too much of an attraction to be accepted with ease.'

The few true friends they have they try to keep in contact with, but rarely do they have people outside of family to their home on social visits and that includes the showbusiness fraternity. Equally rarely do they go to other people's party gatherings. 'I suppose from my point of view I socialize consistently through my work and so that is enough. When I am home I therefore make use of the peaceful hours – I find them refreshing.'

The most activity their home sees is when a particular

family event occurs, such as the christening of their two grandchildren. For this the family gathered in force, friends came over and there was a party mood in the house. 'Joan and I are private people and so naturally enjoy our privacy. This has only been invaded for good reason. For instance, when Gail and Paul set off on their safari. This was in 1975, and we had a large household staying. There were ten others going with them across Africa, starting out from the paddock at our house in three Land Rovers. People seemed to be milling everywhere, half of them I didn't even know. But that was a rather special occasion and such "open house" days are few and far between. I hope it doesn't make me sound unfriendly and unapproachable, because I am not like that at all. I am just a person who enjoys peace and tranquillity when he is able to achieve it.'

DEAR ~~DAD~~ DAD,

IT SEEMS I HAVE ACCIDENTALLY CHANGED THE NAME OF MY HOUSE — OR AT
LEAST MY ABORTIVE EFFORTS AT TYPING HAVE. EVERYTHING SEEMS TO BE
PROGRESSING NICELY AND SO I ENCLOSE ANOTHER CHUNK TO BE CHEWED OVER
WITH BY Y OUR GOOD SELF.

HOPING ALL IS WELL WITH THE FAMILY — I LOOK FORWARD TO CATCHING
UP WITH YOU ALL. TRACEY IS KEEPING WELL AND WORK IS EVER INCREASING.

LOVE AS ALWAYS,

Ofay.

DEAR GARY,

AS YOU CAN SEE FROM THE ABOVE ADDRESS I'VE MOVED. IT WAS NICE
SEEING YOU THE OTHER DAY, IT MADE STEVEN'S DAY, IT WORKS OUT
THAT YOU MAKE STEVEN'S DAY, TRACY MAKES YOUR DAY, I MAKE THE
TAX MANS DAY AND YOUR MOTHER MAKES THE BEDS.

I THINK THE BOOK
IS BETTER FOR THE CUTS AND WE ALL HOPE IT DOES WELL. IT SEEMS
TO HAVE TAKEN A LONG TIME TO DO.

HAVE A NICE HOLIDAY. YOUR
MOTHER SENDS HER LOVE BUT NO MONEY, WHILE I SEND YOU MY LOVE
BUT NO MONEY. SEE YOU BOTH WHEN YOU GET BACK.

LOVE.

XXX

8

Hobbies

I have never been able to understand or appreciate the pleasure obtained by casting a hook and line in the direction of a silent stream of water. Perhaps I am envious that so many people can gain so much enjoyment from what, on initial observation, could be considered a rather mundane and perhaps pointless pastime. What beguiles me further is the appeal this sport holds over all generations. My brother Steven is as fanatical a fisher as our father. They do not fish together very often, because when Dad fishes he enjoys adult company, or just his own. The day before a fishing trip you can see him in the back garden at home, practising his casting and reeling in with an imaginary fish. He packs up the boot of his car with long green wellies, pork pie hat and an old, favourite brown checked jacket that is fractionally on the small side.

His fishing is mainly confined to spots such as the Kennet which he has visited with one of our closest family friends, the highly successful and talented Hertfordshire artist Gordon Benningfield. Gordon is specifically a painter with water colours. His work can range from the intricacies of a butterfly balancing on a dandelion to a large, aggressive white owl. Some of his paintings were featured a few years ago on the television series 'Look Stranger', which involved his friendship with my father and the sharing of their country interests.

As a close friend of the family, and a fishing companion to my father, I asked Gordon if he had any memories from the hours they had spent in each other's company. 'A memory that immediately springs to mind,' he recalled, 'has to be the first time your father kindly invited me to go fishing with him on the River Kennet. To create the right picture, I must introduce your father by saying how extremely and genuinely interested he is in the countryside. And that is not just from a landscape point of view. His love goes deep into the wildlife that can be seen, and he is in fact a life member of the British Butterfly Conservation Society. This means that when we go out together we share a common interest, although our everyday lives are not linked in any specific form. I have a picture that I painted several years ago which depicts a water vole sitting on a branch that is just leaning into the water, causing a gentle ripple. Your father was with me when I first spotted the vole. I nudged him and he took an instant interest, as we decided it resembled an old man in an armchair, with its shoulders hunched and body motionless. This wild animal had all the animation of *The Wind in the Willows* or a Disney creation. These are the sort of moments we share together.

'Anyway, this fishing trip on the Kennet was, excepting one previous time a while back when I was fortunate enough to fish on the Dee at Balmoral, the most exclusive one I had had. As you can possibly imagine, I was somewhat nervous about the prospect, but not to the extent that I was going to turn down this great chance. So, with Eric at the wheel of the car, we headed off to that particularly beautiful part of the country. As we approached the river, the thing that astounded me was the almost ornamental surroundings in which we were to fish. Suddenly I was confronted with sharply-cut lawns with trim, rectangular hedges boxing them in, and along the river at regular intervals were what seemed to be park benches. This all added formality to what to me was normally an informal pastime. When I usually go fishing I find myself wading through lengths of wild grass and spasmodically buried by overhanging weeds and dense thistle. Out here there were few distractions, which meant there were fewer ways for me to fumble around and disguise my inability to fish with any credible professionalism. Other than the presence of your father, I hoped and prayed we would be left alone. So there was your father with his usual eagerness and professionalism, striding deliberately forward, inhaling and exhaling the pure air, with me lumbering loosely behind him like a disturbed Uriah Heep.'

Firstly they visited the club house where, amongst other things, the weighing of the fish is carried out. They generally relaxed and made light conversation with some of the other members, before deciding that they should really head on to the river bank, and have a go at fishing themselves. Inevitably Dad was recognized by the 'gillie' – that is, the river keeper – who approached them at a leisurely pace brandishing a bottle of white wine and two glasses. Gordon picks up the story. 'The gillie smiled, saying, "Nice to see you, Mr Morecambe," and your father acknowledged him and introduced me. Rather typically of him, he couldn't settle for just saying this is Gordon Benningfield; he had to create a story about me. "This is a good friend of mine called Gordon," he began. "He is a remarkable man, he owns two mansions in Scotland and three in Sussex." And of course, everyone believes what your father says when he speaks with such seriousness and authority. I gently smiled and offered a feeble hand, feeling my face turning red. Then, to my horror, your father continued to speak. "Gordon was runner up to the world fly-fishing champion last year, you know."

' "Really!" exclaimed the gillie, looking at me in an altogether different light. "Maybe we will see a thing or two today, then?"

'I think I could have throttled your father at that point.

However, after this awful and I assure you fictitious introduction was over, the gillie left us with two glasses and the wine, and bidding us well he strolled off along the river.

'This really could not have been nicer; just relaxing along the bank with the morning sun shining in our faces and a bottle of wine to enjoy. We consumed the wine very quickly, and on an empty stomach as mine was, this was not a sensible thing to have done. Without doubt, before much time had passed, your father, and especially myself, were feeling the worse for wear. I am not a drinker at the best of times so I was sitting on the bank gently swaying with a glazed expression on my face. Between the two of us we managed to break the glasses, which was a poor show on such a one-off splendid occasion. But we endeavoured to appear sober if nothing else. We pulled ourselves together, realizing that we must get down to some fishing, but appreciating our less-than-capable state. And both of us being non-swimmers, the fishing would have to be carried out at a safe distance from the water's edge. If Eric had fallen in, I don't think I could have hoisted him out, and if I had fallen in, he would certainly have not considered trying to hoist me out. In the end, he limped off one way and I the other, to give ourselves some much-needed room. I am convinced that if there had been any other members in our vicinity that day, I would have been ordered to leave, most probably barred for life. I was fishing everywhere but in the river. The fly had entangled itself around my feet, and then having freed myself from its clasp, I managed to attach it to the bench which was unfortunately behind me.

'Meanwhile your father was giving the appearance of a true professional. Standing twenty or thirty yards to my right, and being the great actor that he is, he could have passed for a world champion fly-fisher that day. His action was so marvellous that I felt like just sitting back and watching him. While he was having much success in catching the fish, I had gathered a bird's nest on my line, which is an obvious term used when enormous knots gather on the line due chiefly to bad casting. During all the chaos and complications, by some miraculous wonderment, I reeled in my line to find that a fish had seemingly jumped on to the hook. Although deserving no credit for my good fortune, I had caught a two-pound rainbow trout.

'At the end of the day your father had not only caught more fish than I would have done if I had stayed out there all year, but he was just choosing the ones he fancied and the others went back into the river. In my excitement I showed him the one and only fish that I had landed. "Look, Eric, I've caught a fish. What do you think?"

' "Oh yes! Well done. I've a few here and a few over there, but there's a big one swimming deep down there I might go after in a minute."

'We wandered back to the car and despite my tiredness I felt thoroughly satisfied by a day out on the Kennet. A day in your father's company I will never forget.'

The other vivid memory that Gordon has of my father rather contrasts with the previous one as it stems from events shortly before he was due to undergo the heart operation. This was some years after their first fishing trip together, and so not only had they become great fishing partners, but they had also developed a close fondness and friendship with one another. Dad's phone call and subsequent visit so close to such a major and traumatic event made him feel very nervous. 'That is, I was very nervous for him,' adds Gordon. 'Whether he was unduly nervous I could not tell, as he is a master at disguising his true feelings. He certainly didn't appear to be nervous as he turned up at my house for a spot of fishing on the river that winds just past my garden. As the day wore on a group of cows trudged over from the nearby meadow, and almost as if they knew who this great man was, started to encircle him. This produced a rather magical moment for me, the outsider looking in. Your father was standing in the centre of these lumbering creatures, with his large Polaroid glasses on, and with fishing rod in hand he pretended to sword fence them off, using the rod as a sword. Fortunately I had my camera with me, and so managed to reel off a few shots. At one stage all I could see was his fly rod wavering unsteadily above the large nodding

Gordon Benningfield's photos of Dad . . .

. . . a day out before the heart operation.

heads, and I remember vividly feeling painfully saddened by the thought of what your father was about to undergo. I just hoped that one day I would see him outside on the river, fooling around like this once again. The whole concept of that day – the fact that he wished to go fishing at this time, and the fact that I felt privileged to share those precious moments with him – is why I remember it as though it were just yesterday. Looking at the matter with cold reality, I honestly felt that this was probably the last time I would be with him, and that all I would have left would be the memories of our days out together. When we said goodbye that evening he gently lowered himself into his car, saying, "We will have to leave it at that for a while, Gordon, but I will see you again in a few months." And of course, he *was* back in a few months, and seems younger and fitter now than at any other time I can recall. What gives me so much personal enjoyment from our friendship, is that he knows there are no formalities when he is with me. He can behave and do exactly what he wants (and believe me he does), without any of the pomp and ceremony that surround him in his normal, complicated life. This relaxed physical and mental state he enjoys when with me is very contagious and adds much pleasure to our all-too-few hours spent together in the country.'

Gordon's most humorous recollection relates back to the river, when the BBC were filming a documentary that he was to appear in. Gordon was on the river at his home again, holding a fishing rod and trying to look fairly professional for the cameras. He was having much difficulty in actually catching any fish. It reached the point of desperation when the producer suggested that someone should rush down to the nearest village and buy a fish to stick on the end of his line. As the idea was considered, Gordon was growing more and more frustrated with his marked lack of success. At that moment a tweed-clad figure appeared in the distance. Gordon takes up the story: 'This figure I recognized as your father. He had come to do a spot of fishing by himself, and, without showing any recognition of me, sat on the opposite bank to the camera crew and prepared himself to fish. The last person the BBC would have expected to turn up on a peaceful Hertfordshire river bank was Eric Morecambe, and I had no intention of telling them. When they asked me who it was fishing opposite, I replied, "Oh, it's just another fisherman who comes down here from time to time."

'He was temporarily forgotten as I persevered in my efforts to land a fish. Meanwhile, equal to my lack of success, your father was having much success. He was reeling in fish after fish, and it had not gone unnoticed by my company. I was beginning to feel a slight unease, perhaps accentuated by my knowing who the happy fisherman was.

'Typically of your father, he could not resist finally crossing the water and heading towards us. As he approached he smiled and said, "Hello, Gordon, how are you getting on?"

As soon as he spoke all faces spun round in sudden recognition, and for one split second time seemed to stand still. In delayed unison they said, "Good God, it's Eric Morecambe!" This out-of-the-blue appearance was quite some bonus for them.

'A few days later I watched a run-through of the programme, and as it reached the end, I could be seen talking to your father whose back was towards the cameras. And at the very end he slowly turned round, removed his glasses and chuckled in his easy, recognizable manner. That was all he needed to do for everyone watching the programme to know who he was.'

Bird-watching, cameras, video-tape machines, clocks and watches and art are all among my father's basic interests. Each of these have held a particular fascination for him at some point over the last fifteen years or so. Other than bird-watching, in which he maintains a constant level of interest in the same manner as fishing, his first noticeable interest is in photography. This usually reaches its peak when he is on holiday, naturally enough. He has taken some fair pictures, but he would be the first to agree that he is by no means a great photographer. His enthusiasm however goes some way to compensate his lack of skill. If there is a photo to take, Dad will be there, reeling off twenty or more shots.

In 1975 I hitch-hiked across Europe with Bill Drysdale and a friend called Phil Watkins. We had spent a few days in the south of France, which proved to be far too expensive for us, we visited Ibiza, from there we crossed to Spain, then we jumped a cattle train and headed for the Algarve where

Three new hats and a new camera.

my parents were at the villa. In Faro we bartered with the taxi driver and for a free drink and sandwich he gave us a cheap fare to Albufeira. As the cab pulled sharply to a halt at the end of the garden, I could see my mother soaking up the sun while reading a book and Dad in a white string vest and a pair of checked baggy shorts, with binoculars hanging loosely around his neck.

He spotted us and as if we were some rare species of birds he had discovered, he raised his glasses and focused on our tired, drawn faces. As we heaved our rucksacks up the garden path, with dust drifting from our bodies with every step, Dad suddenly let out a yell of delight. 'Wha hey!' he nudged my mother. 'Look! It's the boys.' The camera magically appeared from nowhere, and David Bailey was in business. Bill looked at me with a tired smile and said, 'Typical of your Dad. He is the only person who would think of taking a picture when we are gasping for a glass of water.'

We collapsed on to some wooden seats, and it was my mother who went to fetch us some water. We had not had a substantial meal for four or five days, and our noses relished the smell of crispy bacon, fried eggs, chips and toast that soon came drifting out of the kitchen to the patio. So there we all were, sitting round a wrought-iron table with plates laden with home cooking, but eating it was the hard part, as Dad then insisted on showing us all the pictures he had taken so far on their holiday. In turn we had to pass each one of the fifty or more photos around the table muttering how good we thought they were, but in fact completely distracted by the delicious smells of food.

His latest love is video recorders and here we see the boy who never grew up. Gadgets and electrical equipment have always held some spell over him. Perhaps because of his generation and background, he seems unquenchably excited by technological advances. He has in recent months managed to acquire a tape machine with a built-in television and radio. To illustrate his great love for these items, he must be one of the very few people that can switch this built-in television on and at the same time have the main room television on, tuned to a totally different programme. With his video machine he had go a step further by taping a programme while he floats around the house killing time until it is finished, and then he will rewind the tape and sit and watch whatever he has just recorded!

The initial idea behind purchasing the video machines was so we could form a collection of the Morecambe and Wise Shows. Although the videos only date back to 1970, he has reel-to-reel tapes of Morecambe and Wise Shows as far back as the early sixties' ATV series. Guest artists such as the Beatles crop up on these recordings.

Dad has an artistic appreciation of paintings but he is no great collector. Unlike me, he is also quite a good artist himself. His previously unknown talent came to life when he received an art set for a birthday present from Harry Secombe. This was just after we had moved to Hertfordshire and his interest in art suddenly reached a peak. When he was not working he would lock himself away in his study for many hours with such a wide collection of brushes that I think even Picasso would have been jealous. His everyday masterpiece would be a still-life of fruit or a wine bottle — genuinely of a fairly high standard — but on one particular afternoon, after one of his long creative sessions, he appeared from the study holding a canvas that was completely black.

'Well, what do you think?' he asked us.

'What is it?' we inquired.

'It's a coloured man eating a box of liquorice allsorts in a tunnel.'

(WELL THIS IS IT!)

GOOD READING AND CONTACT ME SOON,

LOVE

43, BONDI BEACH TERRACE.

BONDI BEACH,

NEW SOUTH WALES,

AUSTRAILIA.

DEAR GARY,

SO THE BOOK, IF THATS WHAT YOU'VE BEEN WRITING IS FINISHED, GOOD, I'M GLAD FOR YOUR

SAKE. ITS BEEN A LONG HARD STINT FOR YOU, I ONLY HOPE IT WORKS OUT WELL. DONT BE

UPSET IF IT DOESN'T SELL. I'M NOT SURE THAT ANYONE WILL BE THAT INTERESTED IN

ERIC MORECAMBE, EVEN THIS MORNING YOUR MOTHER KEPT CALLING ME ERNIE. I LIKE THE BOOK

AND I'D BUY A COPY IF ITS FREE. ITS A GREAT THRILL FOR ME TO HAVE A BOOK WRITTEN

THATS ALL ABOUT A PERSON I LOVE AND ADMIRE.

I'VE JUST FINISHED A BOOK AND ITS TAKEN

ME THREE MONTHS WHICH GOES TO SHOW WHAT A SLOW READER I AM. KEEP WRITING, I THINK

YOU HAVE A STYLE. THE IMPORTANT THING IS TO WRITE AS MUCH AS YOU CAN AND   TO LISTEN

TO WHAT PEOPLE SAY ABOUT YOUR WORK THEN IGNORE THEM AND DO THE THING YOU WANT   TO

DO. REMEMBER THE OLD SAYING ' IF ALL ABOUT YOU ARE LOSING THEIR HEADS, YOU WILL BE

THE TALLEST PERSON IN THE ROOM. ANYWAY LOVE, GOOD LUCK.

LOVE TO TRACY,

LOVE,

xxx

9

Questions and Answers

I have noticed that whenever I read anything biographical, there is always a great deal more I wish to know that the writer never supplies. There is often a whole area of material missing, a failing that could easily be remedied by a series of direct questions, extracting direct answers. I am certain that a stronger character portrait could be created were such questions asked and the answers printed. I have, therefore, sat my father down with a glass of Perrier water and a Havana cigar and, with list in hand, asked him just a few of the obvious and less obvious questions that I feel, were I not a member of his family, I would wish to have answered.

Gary: I can recall a few of Sadie's stories of your childhood. Can you enlighten us with any more?

Eric: I remember making an inkwell at school during woodwork lessons – we didn't call them carpentry lessons in those days, you know. I could have been no older than seven or eight. This inkwell that I proudly presented to my parents was in fact just a plain lump of wood with a hole skewered in the middle. You couldn't have put any ink in it. It was terrible! But my mother thought it was brilliant. 'Oh, lovely, Eric,' she said, when I gave it to her. Then she called my Dad. 'Look, George. Come and see what our Eric has made.' She actually kept it, along with many similar items throughout her lifetime.

I remember once going with the family on a picnic to Hest Bank. I was ten at the time but I really remember it as though it was this morning. I would have to wear a blazer suit if I was going to look my best. That was short blue flannel trousers and a blue flannel jacket. We were standing at the bus stop waiting to go home when a thunderstorm started and it poured down with rain. The whole of my suit seemed to become sponge-like, soaking up the rain as it fell. I began wiping the rain from my face and hands and legs with my jacket sleeves, but it wasn't just rain – it was blue dye pouring out of my suit. By the time I got home I was blue from head to foot.

I often have a chuckle to myself when I recollect some of my father's endeavours. There was a time when I was a boy when I would sit and watch him catch starlings. He used a dustbin lid and a stick with a piece of string connected to it. Then he would put a lump of bread under the lid and use the stick to support it. When the starling went to have a nibble, he would pull the string and trap the poor little thing. He would catch between ten and twenty of these birds, kill them, then give them to my Auntie Maggie to bake in a pie. She needed about twenty because when you pluck a starling you're not looking at too much flesh. I once had an air gun when I was a lad and he borrowed it to shoot a seagull off our neighbour's roof. He hit it cleanly enough, but it toppled straight down their chimney pot and into the fireplace round which the family were gathered at the time. That must have given them some shock.

Gary: Was there any conversation you had with either parents that later on in life bore any relevance?

Eric: I can recall walking with my mother by the river that weaves its way through Hest Bank. I was fifteen, and she turned to me and said, 'Now one day you'll be a big star, as long as you don't get big-headed. But when you are a big star, you will buy me a house in Hest Bank, won't you?'

I nodded dumbly, and said, 'Yes, Mom, I'll buy you a house out here.'

Many years later, in the latter part of the sixties, whenever I saw her she would say, 'Well you *are* a big star, and now where's my house you promised me at Hest Bank?' And eventually I bought her a home in Hest Bank.

Gary: Were you successful in talent competitions during your youth?

Eric: George had eleven brothers and it's only now that I realize it was possibly because of them that I won every single talent show in Morecambe! They would all come and watch and start leaping out of their seats cheering and clapping at me, at the end of my spot. They would also bring their families with them, so you're talking about thirty-five people in the audience all showing biased appreciation towards me. I don't think the judges would have dared let me lose! I entered nearly fifteen competitions and won every single one of them. The nigger minstrels (if still in existence, they would, I imagine, be known as the black and white minstrels) who performed on the beach at Morecambe actually barred me from entering their talent contests after I won three times in a row. They probably barred my relatives as well.

Gary: What is your earliest living memory?

Eric: No one ever believes this but my mother would have always verified it for me. My earliest recollection is of when I was nine months old. I remember being put on the kitchen table in our home in Buxton Street, to be wrapped in a coat and long scarf before being taken out in my pushchair. I can also remember that the roof of that house had caved in, and that was why we were the first on the list to be moved to Christie Avenue by the council.

Gary: How long have the Bartholomews lived in Lancashire?

Eric: I only know as far back as my great-grandfather on my Dad's side, who brought his family to Lancashire from what was then Westmorland but is now Cumbria. So we have been Lancastrians for approximately a hundred and fifty years or so. By coincidence, my grandparents on my mother's side were also from Westmorland, but came down some years afterwards.

Gary: At the risk of encouraging letters of complaint and concern, what are your feelings about religion?

Eric: I am basically not a religious person. I cannot say that I have genuinely turned to it as a real source of comfort or inspiration, at least, not knowingly. Although in essence I do not believe in the one God that is proffered by the Bible, I live with a slight unease that perhaps He does exist. But that is a commonsense attitude. What I hope I will not do, when I reach about seventy or so – *if* I reach seventy or so – is, in panic and fear in the lessening years I have, turn to it then and enact the life of a God-fearing Christian. To me that would be like cramming for your finals. Not that it is applicable to me, I hope, but if you go all the way through life drinking and smoking and generally abusing yourself and perhaps others, it seems rather unChristian and hypocritical to turn to God in old age, and say, 'Well, I've had a good time, I suppose now I had better repent.' At the moment I don't, or rather don't try, to believe in a God and a creator, but I would not interfere or knock anyone that does believe. I would also add that I may change my opinions. I certainly believe in the laws of Christianity. The world would be a better place to live in if more people kept to the Ten Commandments.

Gary: And similarly with politics?

Eric: No, I am not politically motivated. Actually, I am one of those terrible people (along with ninety-nine per cent of the country) who wants his politics to run no deeper than pushing for more money and as little tax as possible. As for the party in power, I am unconcerned as long as they can help fill this need.

Gary: On a safer note, how extreme is your taste in music?

Eric: Extreme to the full. I enjoy all kinds of music. I adore jazz and swing, straight and even some of the pop music. Of late I have developed a taste for Country and Western. I was always a fan of Roger Miller and now I collect Dolly Parton and Tammy Wynette.

In the jazz field, Duke Ellington, Count Basie and Glen Miller are the greats to me. I slipped up when I was a youngster. I was working in a theatre in Liverpool doing pantomime and Duke Ellington was due shortly to appear there. It happened to be that he was going to use the same dressing-room that I was in. I left him a short note saying, 'Please help yourself to drink,' and so forth. He wrote me a lovely reply, being the kind man that he was, saying, 'Hi there, thanks for the room and the drink, great being in your room, Eric,' and so on, and signed it the Duke. And I lost the damn thing. *And* I didn't get round to going to see his show, which is something I should have done. During the war Irving Davies, the choreographer, took me along to the Corn Exchange in Bedford to see Glen Miller recording. That was a big thrill for a seventeen-year-old lad, as I then was.

Gary: Is there anyone in particular in the music world that you have not met and would wish to meet?

Eric: Not individually, no. I have met many of the ones that *I* consider great. André Previn, Yehudi Menuhin and so on. Perhaps I am accustomed to it, but it is no big thrill in meeting them as, like myself, they are ordinary people. It is only their talent that makes them anything but ordinary people. I believe that it is the ones with the lesser talent who try to be something they are not. They go a little round the twist in the end. Anyone that can't handle it shouldn't be allowed it; sex included.

Gary: Keeping the music theme in mind, how interested (not so much from a self-performing point of view) are you in song and dance and musicals?

Eric: Well, I would honestly prefer to stay in and watch a Fred Astaire and Ginger Rogers film than go out to a party. I look upon that, and its kind, as pure, out-and-out entertainment, something I sadly feel is dying in the celluloid world of today. The magic has gone. Everything seems to be more bizarre, perhaps more realistic, but there is little escapism left to the viewer.

Gary: What sports are you interested in (barring Luton from the conversation)?

Eric: There *is* only Luton in sport! No, again I enjoy a fair cross-section, of which cricket leads the list. I like to watch cricket in extreme comfort or on television. I go to every test match held at Lord's, and sit with the chairman and thoroughly enjoy being spoiled.

Gary: What are your feelings on comedians past and present?

Eric: I suppose in my line of profession Laurel and Hardy feature very highly in my admiration. I never had much time for Charlie Chaplin, although I would not deny the fact he was probably a genius. But to me he wasn't as funny as Buster Keaton. But he must have been a better business man, because he made and protected a lot more money than most at that time. Harold Lloyd was a marvellous actor / comic and one of the few who successfully made the transition from the silent movies into sound. That is quite an achievement when you consider people such as Jimmy James, Sid Field, Dave Morris and others of that ilk found it very difficult to perform even on the radio.

Contemporary comics concern me slightly. I worry because I feel there is very little talent coming up, but maybe I am saying that because I am an old pro now. I don't know. Perhaps I envy the fact that the newcomers are young and they have it all to go. I think that inevitably this country will become more like America and that stars will come along and make a small fortune and a big name for themselves, but this will only last for two or three years. After that they will find it difficult to even get themselves arrested.

In the double-act field, I would have thought Cannon and Ball would have a great chance for long-term survival and taking over from Ernie and I. That depends obviously on how they go about it. Firstly they must handle themselves correctly and carefully, which I am sure they do. I have met them once and I found them quite pleasant. Business- and material-wise I have no idea what they are like. Some of the routines they perform are still very weak, but there is much talent there, and with the right assistance it could be tapped. You can reach a certain level in showbusiness, and then after that there are very few that achieve the next step. I hope that Cannon and Ball achieve it. At the risk of leaving out names, I think that Tommy Steele, Mike Yarwood, John Cleese, Tommy Cooper, Dick Emery, Spike Milligan, Jimmy Tarbuck, Roy Castle, Des O'Connor, The Two Ronnies, Morecambe and Wise and all those I have forgotten have made it to that next level. Rowan Atkinson is going that way. He is another of the up-and-coming who may well be at the top for as long as he is working. It is a very special level, because you become more than just accepted and liked; it goes beyond that.

Gary: Who do you admire most in showbusiness?

Eric: It would have to be Arthur Askey, mainly because

of his longevity and that he has survived so long as a star. He must be the Cary Grant of radio.

Gary: Are you a great comedy fan?

Eric: No. I prefer to be at home watching that Fred Astaire and Ginger Rogers film.

Gary: If you could lead your life again, would you wish to change anything?

Eric: No. I would do everything the same – but quicker.

Gary: Would you want to change all those years of touring?

Eric: No. I loved it.

Gary: Would you choose Ernie again as a partner?

Eric: Yes, because there is no one better. I would say he is the greatest straight man in the country. The only thing I suppose I would change would be the illnesses. But even with the health problems, I have had a very fortunate life. I think I have given as well as I have taken. I have never knowingly done anything malicious or vicious in my life. I am basically a soft man, although I will stick up for my rights and I won't suffer fools. But Ernie and I, as an act, always fought back. Before we were stars we were often hammered down, and we would have to say, 'Well, we will prove to you we *are* good,' whether it was to producers or whoever.

Gary: What is your biggest achievement?

Eric: From a professional view, just the fact we have achieved so much. We have become part of British showbusiness history, and that is a wonderful feeling. Of course that leads to the extra achievements, the ones that have to be considered the cream on top of our careers, such as the OBE, Madame Tussauds, and the personality awards. My biggest achievement was being given the doctorate at Lancaster University. That was extra special as it had nothing directly to do with comedy, charity work, or that I support Luton. It was purely their gift to a successful son of Lancashire.

Father comedian

Even in hell where misery /torment fills its own rancid air,
The sorrow of lost faceless souls
Can dare be allowed to lift in one tender moment.
Untimely movements, moments and interruptions
Disappear when the golden wand
Is in the golden touch of the magic performer.
His ageless audience corruption
Stands high as he braves to shine
Where no man has shone before,
But instead, successfully died.

The pride and superiority is held over the real and unreal
    eyes,
From behind his steel-rimmed glasses,
From behind his steel-rimmed mind.
And the spontaneous laughter and tears
Echo joy and fears as the show flows onwards,
Irrepressible in its timeless, coherent passage.

To a smoke and drink filled box,
Entitled 'Dressing Room – Star',
Here the painful swelling and squealing
Of a dull champagne cork
Perpetrates through the haze of social relaxation,
Contentment and hangers-on.
The sweet success and failure,
Only paralleled by heaven and hell itself,
Runs freely from the warm auditorium headstones,
And out into the sweet green pastures

156

Of modern city,
To the highest of highest journalistic boardrooms
To the men who pass fate and judgement
On the performer's sense of humour.
And as,
(In the fashion of the dying soldier
whose friend leans weeping at his bedpost),
Everything must pass on save the performer's sense of
humour.